Women Who Shine

Anointed with fresh oil

Noela Richards

New Wine Press

New Wine Press
PO Box 17
Chichester
England PO20 6YB

ISBN: 1 903725 08 9

Typeset by CRB Associates, Reepham, Norfolk.
Printed in England by Clays Ltd, St Ives plc.

Contents

Introduction

This book was conceived in my heart earlier this year when I spoke at a women's conference in London. Something took place at that event that can only be described as a God happening. Not only were the women who attended forever marked by the Spirit of God, but I was forever marked as He touched me in a new way.

The Lord had impressed upon my heart that the women were to be anointed with oil during the last conference session – that they were to leave with a fresh anointing and we were to believe that as the natural oil was applied, that the oil of the Holy Spirit would be applied. Two instructions were clear – we were to use a new bottle of oil and the convenor of the conference was to be the one to pour the oil upon the women.

I explained to the women what I had sensed the Lord say and then I handed the bottle of oil over to our host. The presence of the Spirit overwhelmed her and she could barely stand under the weight of His being. As she broke the seal on the lid of the bottle she fell over! Oil spilt over the sides of the bottle and onto the floor. Some of the women hurriedly ran out to their cars to look for towels and blankets, and we began to place various materials on the floor. We tried to get our host on her feet, but finally, after much laughter, we left her on the floor, and asked those who desired to be anointed with the oil to come forward.

As the women came they sat or kneeled. Some were anointed on their heads and others on their hands or feet. Oil was poured out liberally. Each person was deeply touched of the Lord, sensing that this was not just something made of man, but truly conceived in God's heart.

I watched as each person came forward and was astonished to see that the level of the oil in the bottle hadn't moved! It was being poured out lavishly – smeared all over the women and yet it hadn't lessened! I turned to the person next to me who had made the same observation. We just looked at each and then back at the bottle. More oil had been poured out than the level in the bottle indicated. We were experiencing an act of God! (As we continued to watch we noted that after some time the level began to decrease.)

As women, God had met with us and we had met with Him. As each of us who were anointed that day glistened with fresh oil, I couldn't help but be challenged by the call to know without reservation that we are anointed of Him – that we should shine for Him everyday of our lives – that we should so carry the anointing within us and upon us that it is evident for all to see.

The anointing is the supernatural ability of God. It is His enabling and His empowering. Christ is the Anointed One, so when we are in Him, we are anointed. We have His ability to live an overcoming victorious Christian life; we have His ability to fulfil a specific call; and we have His ability to be a vital part of the body of Christ.

The Concise English Dictionary defines the word 'anoint' as being to 'smear with oil or ointment' or 'to consecrate with oil'. **We have been anointed**. The fresh oil of the Spirit has been poured out liberally upon our lives to accompany the anointing that abides. Thus, we glisten and our lives shine with His presence. His power works within us and we are enabled to live successfully for Him.

That day as I watched the women being anointed of the Father in a new way, I heard Him speak to me of the fresh anointing that He is desiring to pour out upon women in this hour. This new anointing is an Esther anointing that raises women up to walk in their destinies. This anointing calls and enables the daughters of the Father to rise in courage and faith. It empowers and equips. It releases and blesses. It is a call to stand before the King and intercede on behalf of others to bring deliverance and liberty. This anointing makes a way for others to enter into their spiritual inheritance.

This 'Esther anointing' (see note below) causes women to realise (by revelation) their royal status that has come through the bloodline of Christ. It brings the ability in Him to cast off the beggarly garments of the earth – the garments of the past, as well as the garments of experience, and accept the royal robes of the household of the Sovereign Lord.

God doesn't make junk and He doesn't make mistakes. He has fashioned you in love and He wants you to really understand who He is to you and who you are in Him. He has called you to be successful in every endeavour of life; He has called you to be more than a conqueror in the private areas of heart and mind; and He has called you to be victorious in spirit! I have written this book to let you know you have been called to be **a woman who shines**.

Let Him anoint you afresh.

Noela Richards

Note: The 'Esther anointing' is a particular manifestation of the Holy Spirit and His power that is being released in the earth today to raise up women to their calls. There are times when God manifests particular aspects of the anointing for particular purposes such as the healing anointing, the restoration anointing, the financial anointing and the prophetic anointing.

Chapter 1

They Shall Reign in Life

> *'For if by one man's offence death reigned by one; much more they which receive abundance of grace and of the gift of righteousness shall reign in life by one, Jesus Christ.'*
> (Romans 5:17 KJV)

Each one of us has been called to 'reign' in life, that is, to have lordship and rulership over our lives under Christ, allowing His life to reign in us. To 'reign' is to live life from a royal position. It is to live life in victory, peace, joy and power. However, this level of spiritual dominion is only possible when every area of our lives is submitted to the Lordship of Christ.

So often we think of the Lordship of Christ over the spiritual aspects of our lives. We dress up on Sunday putting on our 'spiritual clothes' and a smile, and go off to church for worship, fellowship and the Word of God, yet deep inside we know there are areas of life that have never been brought under His Lordship – areas where we can't seem to get the victory – areas we think we have to try and manage as best we can.

God cares about us. He wants us to overcome in every area of life. He doesn't want areas hidden in shame, areas put in the 'too hard' basket, areas stuffed down into our hearts. He wants us to enjoy all of the liberty and victory He purchased for us . . . all of the benefits of the New Covenant.

You know the devil wants areas of failure hidden in the dark places. He wants you to believe you are a failure, and there is no hope. God wants all of our lives 'in the light' – not so He can ridicule, but so that He can do whatever is needed within you to bring you through to victory – so that you will have a testimony to share with others.

Each year I receive letters from women all over the world who are living in defeat and shame. Some have shopping addictions, some have eating disorders, others gamble. All of these are women who love the Lord, but have not yet entered into overcoming faith in particular areas of their lives. When I speak with women I often ask what their lives are like. Many answer with responses like, 'crazy', 'chaotic', or 'out of control'. Some say that they just can't get organised; their homes are messy and their lives are messy; others say they battle with eating disorders; some take tranquilisers to help get them through the day; whilst others have difficulty controlling their tongues.

These ones suffer such shame and often are so fearful that people will find out 'what they're really like'. Feelings of guilt and failure overtake them. Condemnation settles around their lives. It feels like the harder they try to overcome, the more ground they lose – and there are thousands upon thousands of women in the world who feel like this. Self-rejection rules over them, as they feel increasingly worthless.

Scripture makes it clear that God holds victory in store for the upright (see Proverbs 2:7 NIV). This means that God has stored up for you and me every piece of victory we will ever need – that is, His ability to overcome in any situation. The Sovereign Lord is above any eating disorder, any addiction, any stronghold and any bad habit. No matter what it is that you don't feel able to overcome, He has the answer. He has the strategy for release. He has the keys to healing. **He has the victory**.

So, instead of trying unsuccessfully (or with partial success) to overcome, release the area of difficulty to God – confess it and then ask Jesus to take up Lordship over that area and then let Him minister to you so that you are able to walk in dominion in that part of your life. Never again feel condemned, never again feel a failure, start to enter into His victory!

When you make Jesus Lord of any area, you give Him permission to begin to pull that area into **Divine alignment**. The word 'align' means to 'bring into line or agreement'. So, rather than condemnation, you will feel conviction about this area. You will start to see the problem as He sees it – in the light of the Word. And, as He pulls this area into line with His will He will bring the revelation needed to strengthen you, He will bring the strategy needed to cause you to walk free (and stay free) and He will even begin to change your desires to good, godly, healthy desires!

He won't just pick the fruit, He'll pull out the root. He'll sow within you the seed of His Word and it will produce righteousness. In the very area of life that has seemed so difficult, His glory will shine!

Below I have listed out some of the areas that women seem to struggle with most. I challenge you to look down the list and place a tick near the areas of life that you know need to be brought into Divine Order – so that you can reign! (I have not divided these issues into categories of body, soul and spirit, because, in fact, all of these issues are spiritual.)

Addictions, compulsive behaviour and false comforts

- ☐ Wasting time shopping
- ☐ Over-spending
- ☐ Eating disorders
- ☐ Gambling

Disorganisation

- ☐ Clutter
- ☐ Hoarding
- ☐ Waste

Time issues

- ☐ Always late
- ☐ Running out of time
- ☐ Wasting time
- ☐ Don't make good use of time

Fantasy

- ☐ Avoiding reality
- ☐ Wishing you were someone else
- ☐ Romantic fantasy
- ☐ Sexual fantasy

Self-rejection

- ☐ Hatred of self
- ☐ Poor diet
- ☐ Lack of exercise

Money issues

- ☐ Poverty thinking
- ☐ Deepening debt
- ☐ Difficulty in giving and receiving

Heart issues

- ☐ Gossip
- ☐ False accusation
- ☐ Jealousy
- ☐ Criticism
- ☐ Live in fear

- ☐ Anger
- ☐ Impatience
- ☐ Easily offended

Devotional life issues

- ☐ Little time in the Word
- ☐ Little time in prayer
- ☐ Not aware of God's presence daily
- ☐ Feel condemned
- ☐ Lack of faith
- ☐ God will do it for others, but not for me

Now – take the time to pray:

> 'Father, Your Word says in Proverbs 2 that You have victory stored up for me. But, in this area of my life [speak it out] I have not been living in victory. So, today, I bring this area and I surrender it to You. I bring it into the light and give this area over to You. In the name of Jesus I will no longer allow it mastery over me. I break the power of the lie that has kept me in slavery to this thing. No longer will I live in disorder, shame and guilt. By Your grace I will enter into Your victory.
>
> Father, I ask You to bring this area of my life into Divine alignment with Your heart and will. I ask You to do all that You need to do in me to enable me to walk in dominion and liberty. Bring me the revelation of the Word that I need, the anointing that I need and all of the practical assistance I need to live in overcoming faith in this area. This day I ask You to release a strategy from heaven that will set me free. Amen.'

Take communion and declare that because of the blood of Christ you are a covenant woman. Ask the Father to show you how to appropriate every blessing of the covenant you have with Him. By faith receive all that you need to walk in the blessings He has for you. Then begin to worship Him declaring His greatness. Spend some time in His presence and let Him minister to you.

Chapter 2

I Have Considered My Ways

> *'I have considered my ways and have turned my steps to your statutes.'* (Psalm 119:59 NIV)

In the first chapter of *Women Who Shine* we considered our ways. We looked honestly at the areas of our lives that have not been placed under the Lordship of Christ, **and** we turned our steps toward His statutes. We made a decision of heart and mind to go God's way, and therefore, to reign over, rather than be ruled over!

We made a decision to walk differently – to follow after His statutes. What is a statute? It is simply a written law. Therefore, we have made the decision to walk the way of the Word. We do this in two ways: firstly, by studying what the Word says about the area of life that has kept us in slavery. (This shows us God's perspective on the matter and presents us with truth. It gives us the opportunity to deal with wrong thinking and prepares us to walk in liberty.) John 8:31–32 says:

> *'...If ye continue in my word, then are ye my disciples indeed; And ye shall know the truth, and the truth shall make you free.'* (KJV)

And, secondly, by making the Word first place in our lives. This is accomplished by observing a plan to spend time in the Scriptures daily. We should be sowing the Word into our lives everyday, so that we can expect a harvest of righteousness.

You know, I can almost hear what many of you are thinking right now. This woman wants me to find more time in my day! You must be kidding. Well, I'm not kidding. Hearing and obeying the Word places a foundation under your life that will keep you in victory during tough times (see Matthew 8:24–27). And, there is only one way to build yourself strong in God – and that is by feeding on the Word.

Prayerfully set a realistic goal of the amount of time or chapters you feel God would have you read each day. Start to think about your schedule and cut away the unnecessary (the unnecessary is anything that doesn't profit your life). Consider breaking up your devotional time – e.g. read the Word for 10 or 15 minutes a few times a day.

Start a program. Read some of the Old Testament and some of the New; or say three chapters of the Old Testament, three chapters of the New, five Psalms and one chapter of Proverbs. Whatever works for you! You can begin small and work up. You can carry a small Bible in your purse and when you're waiting for the kids or are in some situation where you are required to wait you can read a bit.

There are all sorts of variations you can make to 'Word time'. The important thing to remember is that you are an individual. Your life is unlike that of anyone else around you. I promise that if you make reading the Word a priority in your life, then the Lord will start to give you creative ideas as to how to spend this precious time with Him.

One thing that works for me . . . usually I spend December of every year at home in Brisbane. I wind down for the year and prepare for the next year. During this time I endeavour to read the gospels four times in that month. I work out how many chapters it will take to accomplish my goal and then get up a little earlier . . . and throughout that month I feast on the Word. This prepares me for the new year:

- It cleanses me and renews my mind.
- It positions me in the Spirit.
- It gives me a storehouse of Scripture from which to minister.

You know, there are all sorts of ways you can feed on the Word. You can watch videos of powerful preaching when you're ironing or you can listen to teaching tapes when you're cooking. In fact, I listen to the Word nearly all day. I have a tape player by my bed so that I can hear the Word as I fall asleep. I keep a tape player in my bathroom so that as I shower and get ready for the day I can listen to the Word. I keep a tape player in my kitchen . . . and also in the car.

You may think that you have no time for the Word, but actually if you seek God, He will give you creative ways to spend time in the Scriptures.

You know, I've found that if I give time to God, He gives time to me. What do I mean by that? I mean that when I honour Him by spending time in His Word – getting to know Him and letting Him speak to me, then somehow all the other things that I need to do get taken care of!

In fact, you may have a friend that will embark on some type of reading plan with you, so that you can encourage each other along the way.

It may seem when you first start your reading program, that it is just so hard, but if you persevere you will find that you become addicted to the Word and what it produces in your life. You can't do with it. You'll find that because you are **seeking first the kingdom** – every other area of your life will begin to fall into right order.

When we make the Word first place, we give the Spirit of God an opportunity to speak to us and realign areas that are out of order. We come under conviction as we are challenged by the power of the Word because the Word is alive.

It is the Word of God and it separates – it separates between soul and spirit. It discerns and exposes our thoughts, beliefs and heart motives. Hebrews 4:12 says:

> *'For the word of God is quick, and powerful, and sharper than any two-edged sword, piercing even to the dividing asunder of soul and spirit, and of the joints and marrow, and is a discerner of the thoughts and intents of the heart.'*
> (KJV)

The Word cleanses us. It renews our thinking. It changes the way we see life because it challenges the paradigms we hold through culture and experience. It builds within us the principles and ways of God. The Word causes us to see as God sees.

The Word of God causes our inner man to be strengthened. It silences our soul man and allows our regenerated spirit man to rise up to the leadership of our lives. We are no longer motivated by the flesh. We are led of the Spirit – motivated by a desire to please God.

When Joshua was commissioned to lead the Israelites into the Promised Land, the Lord gave him the instruction to **continually speak the Word, do the Word and meditate upon the Word** (see Joshua 1:8). This was Joshua's success strategy – and it is our success strategy for every endeavour of life!

- **Speak the Word**. Start to speak Scripture. Pray Scripture. Sing Scripture. Praise and worship with Scripture. Let His Word fill your mouth!
- **Do the Word**. Whatever you see in the Word – do! By faith start to be a hearer and doer.
- **Meditate upon the Word**. Think about what you're reading. Ask God what it means and to speak to you from it. The Concise English Dictionary says that to 'meditate' is to be 'occupied in thought'. Write scriptures out and place them before your eyes – on the

refrigerator, on mirrors, on your desk, even on the dashboard of your car. Place scriptures on cards and put them in your wallet or pocket. Carry the Word always! Meditation causes the Word to go deep down into your heart. It changes your heart.

I'm a city girl and know very little about the country, but I'm told a cow will chew grass, swallow it and then later bring it up – only to chew on it again. As this process is repeated over and over the grass becomes broken down or refined, and more of the goodness of the grass is assimilated into the stomach of the cow. You know, the more you chew over Scripture, the more it is broken down, so that revelation can become part of your being. The truth of the Scripture actually becomes part of you – your heart and your mind.

Someone once told me that meditation also means 'to mutter'. The dictionary says that to 'mutter' is 'to speak with the mouth nearly closed'. I've made it a habit to mutter Scripture every time I get in the car to drive – even if it's for a short trip.

Memorisation is another key to getting the Word into your heart. We tell Sunday school children to memorise verses, but somehow as we get older and a little more sophisticated we forget how powerful this can be! We should all be working on some memorisation plan. And, if you say, 'Noela, I have difficulty remembering things', then begin to declare, 'I have the mind of Christ' and start with short scriptures.

So ... make the Word first place ... let it wash you ... let it renew your mind ... let it bring you God's truth ... let it show you who He is.

With the measure you use ...

Mark chapter 4 presents us with some powerful parables which illustrate how the Kingdom of God operates. A parable is a story with a moral lesson. A parable carries a principle or truth. In this particular passage of Scripture we read of: the Parable of the Sower, the Parable of the Growing Seed and the Parable of the Mustard Seed.

The Parable of the Sower is listed first, because it is first. This story and the truths it contains are the chief things a Christian needs to understand to lead a prosperous life through the Word of God. In fact, Jesus said to the ones gathered around Him,

> *'... Don't you understand this parable? How then will you understand any parable?'* (Mark 4:13 NIV)

Jesus was saying that the key to understanding the principles which He shared during His time on earth lay in understanding the truths of this story. So, the Parable of the Sower is of utmost importance, and deserves more than a cursory glance. Every believer needs to meditate upon this parable and seek the Lord for revelation of the truths it contains. After all,

> *'As long as the earth endures, seedtime and harvest ... will never cease.'* (Genesis 8:22 NIV)

The Kingdom operates on the law of seedtime and harvest or as we would commonly term 'sowing and reaping' just as the earth does. And, this law is **the most important law** for the believer to grasp.

The Parable of the Sower tells us how to reap a maximum yield on seed that is sown. Verse 14 speaks of the farmer 'sowing the word'. I talked earlier of sowing the Word into our hearts to reap a harvest. Mark 4 speaks of the importance of the soil being in good condition – ready to receive the seed.

It is up to each one of us to tend our hearts so that we receive seed of the Word that can take root, grow and flourish until harvest time (see Mark 4:14–20). It is up to each one of us to cast every care upon the Lord so that we are 'anxious for nothing', so that the pressures and worries of this life don't choke out the growing Word. It is up to each one of us to ensure that the Lord is kept pre-eminent in our hearts and occupies first place.

> *'Consider carefully what you hear ... With the measure you use, it will be measured to you – and even more. Whoever has will be given more; whoever does not have, even what he has will be taken from him.'* (Mark 4:24, 25 NIV)

Be careful what you hear ... With the measure you use, it will be measured to you – and even more. It may interest you to know that if a group of us were together in a room and someone was speaking, we would not all hear the same thing. Oh, we might hear the same words, but we would not hear the same thing.

Sometimes, after preaching, I've been approached by a person who has come to thank me for ministering on a particular subject. You know, the funny thing is, I don't even remember mentioning that topic. But, that is what the hearer heard!

We don't listen with the flappy things positioned on the sides of our heads. Oh, we are enabled to hear sounds, but we don't **hear** with these organs. We hear with our hearts, we hear with our experiences, we hear with our culture. We hear through the **paradigms** that are in place within us – so what we hear is determined by and received through our mindsets.

'What we hear' and the 'measure we use' or what we hear in our hearts and how we judge or determine what we hear is sown into our lives and we'll reap on what has been sown. For example, if I'm a fearful person, then I'll hear through fear, and fear will be sown into my heart – thus I'll reap more fear.

Let me explain it a simple way ... A paradigm is a model or a mindset or a frame of reference. It is a perspective. It is the way in which we see things, or if you like, it is the glasses through which we see God, ourselves and others. Paradigms are formed within us through upbringing, experiences, education, culture, and even expectations.

Think about the paradigms that have been laid in your life – **the glasses through which you see, hear and receive.**

Romans 12:1, 2 says:

> *'I beseech you therefore, brethren, by the mercies of God, that ye present your bodies a living sacrifice, holy, acceptable unto God, which is your reasonable service. And be not conformed to this world: but be ye transformed by the renewing of your mind, that ye may prove what is that good, and acceptable, and perfect, will of God.'* (KJV)

These verses instruct us to present our 'bodies' (our whole beings) to the Lord; to not be conformed to the world and its images; but, rather, be transformed (or as the dictionary says 'change shape') by the renewing of our minds, so that we will be able to discern and prove the will of God.

We must allow the Word and the Spirit to transform our minds – to challenge us and at times convict us to surrender ungodly mindsets in order to receive His mindsets – His way of thinking and being.

You know, because I'm Australian, I think in Australian social and cultural terms. I see through Australian glasses, but, I realised a long time ago that my God is not Australian (and that not everything in my culture glorifies Him!). So, I have had to lay aside some cultural frames of reference to grow in Him and further take up my heavenly citizenship and receive His mindsets.

John chapter 7 gives an account of a conversation that took place between Christ and some of the religious men of His day. He said to the men,

> *'Stop judging by mere appearances, and make a right judgement.'* (John 7:24 NIV)

You see they were considering Christ through a religious paradigm and therefore when He healed a sick person on the Sabbath they were furious. They would rather argue a point of law then accept a miracle of healing!

- ***How* we see and how we hear is just as important as *what* we see and what we hear!**

I am convinced that there are times when the Father answers our prayers, meets our needs or undertakes for us in miraculous ways – but because of our mindsets (which determine and limit our expectations) we just aren't able to receive what He has done. We aren't able to walk in what He has performed because we just can't 'see' His hand – we can't 'see' why He would do it that way, why He would use those people...

The Lord wants to lay within our minds and hearts paradigms which will cause us to see as He sees and hear as He hears so that we can respond as He responds.

✣ ✣ ✣

> *'Thou art my portion, O LORD: I have said that I would keep thy words. I intreated thy favour with my whole heart: be merciful unto me according to thy word.* ***I thought on my ways, and turned my feet unto thy testimonies****. I made haste, and delayed not to keep thy commandments. The bands of the wicked have robbed me: but I have not forgotten thy law. At midnight I will rise to give thanks unto thee because of thy righteous judgements. I am a companion of all them that fear thee, and of them that keep thy precepts. The earth, O LORD, is full of thy mercy:* ***teach me thy statutes****.'* (Psalm 119:57–64 KJV)

Below I have set out a prayer to help you bring what you have just read before the Lord.

'Lord, I have considered my ways and have turned my steps to Your statutes. I love Your Word and I love Your ways, because they lead to life. Instruct me in Your ways, renew my thinking and change my mind where necessary, so that I can walk in liberty and freedom. Lord, sow truth into my spirit. Give me revelation as I seek You and give me direction as I serve You.

I give You permission to begin to pull down the strongholds of thinking that have been set up in my life that don't glorify You and begin to lay paradigms that will please You. In the name of Jesus. Amen.'

Chapter 3

The Father's Blessing

Last year I spoke at a summer camp in England. For many months before the actual event, I had known by the Spirit that I was to minister on the subject of 'Breaking the Curse of Fatherlessness'. I knew that this was God's message for that meeting. However, I was astounded to see just how many He touched through this Word. Since that time, I have ministered the message in Asia and Australia – with the same results – men and women healed and established in relationship with their Heavenly Father.

I have come to realise that to experience the blessing of the Father upon our lives is just so important. Our whole existence (and salvation) is based on His Father heart.

> *'For God so loved the world, that he gave his only begotten Son, that whosoever believeth in him should not perish, but have everlasting life.'* (John 3:16 KJV)

He sent His son to die for us – to redeem us and to bring us into adoption, that we might be His heirs.

Yet many of us have not been able to relate to God the Father in any great depth. Some of us (because of paradigms) have only thought of God in religious terms – a legalistic and harsh ruler; others have been presented with a poor example of fatherhood; and yet others still have not been fathered at all. This has caused an inability for many people to move into a fruitful relationship with the Heavenly Father.

In fact, fatherlessness (the lack of true fathering) brings a curse. It brings an inability to receive all of the blessings that are meant to come from a father as inheritance. The blessings are cut off; provision is absent; and protection is not in place. Where there should be blessing, there is cursing.

Malachi chapter 4 verses 5 and 6 speak of the curse of fatherlessness. This curse rests upon individuals, churches and even nations. It holds back an entering into and fully possessing the promises of the Father's heart. This curse keeps its captives bound with a continual sense of striving to be good enough; it brings lack and poverty; and it causes a 'works' mentality to operate in every relationship. This curse brings a difficulty in receiving.

As apostolic anointing rises in the earth, God's Father heart will be revealed in an ever-increasing measure, and He will require a response from His children. He will require us to look to Him as the One who watches over us paternally. As we do this, He will draw us in close and there will come greater understanding of the incredible love He has for each one of us.

In the Old Testament we read of the patriarchs laying hands upon their children and blessing them. The word 'bless' can at times throughout Scripture be defined as 'to empower to prosper'. When the fathers of the Old Testament blessed their children they empowered them to prosper. They released them to succeed in life. They released them to do well. Wherever the children went and whatever they did, they knew they had their father's backing and blessing.

The father's blessing not only consisted of laying hands upon the children, but also prophetically speaking over them. This carried such anointing and was so powerful in the spirit realm that the children grew into what their fathers declared! Impartation took place from father to child and a way was made in the Spirit for that child to do well.

Remember, the story in Genesis 27 of Jacob deceitfully taking Esau's blessing. Jacob came before his father pretending to be his brother Esau. So, when Esau presented himself to his father Isaac to receive from him, there really was little for the patriarch to say. When Esau realised that his father had been tricked into giving away his blessing, he loudly cried out, 'Bless me – me too, my father'! (see Genesis 27:34). (The Hebrew people knew that one of the primary functions of the father was to bless his children. It fell to him to name them and prepare them for destiny.)

Most of us have never known the type of fathering that prepares us for destiny. Some people have had fathers that were physically present but emotionally absent; others have had fathers who were only critical and abusive; and sadly some have had fathers who never took up their responsibility to provide for their needs. Through various circumstances, some have never known their fathers.

Every curse has fruit which are outward manifestations of its presence. The fruit of fatherlessness includes a continual seeking for approval and acceptance; feelings of rejection and the fear of rejection loom large in the lives of the fatherless, as they strive to find the love they know is rightfully theirs.

Scripture shows God to be a Father who unconditionally loves, provides for, corrects and trains His kids. But, in the areas in which we've experienced fatherlessness we'll have difficulty believing and receiving His ministry to us. Therefore, it is crucial that we allow Him to heal us (and even to place within us that which was not present in the natural family).

Jabez was a man from a dysfunctional family. His father didn't appear to be on the scene. He was named by his mother (which was not socially and culturally the way of the Israelites). He was called 'pain' – wherever he went and whatever he did he was known as one who caused pain. Yet, he called to the Lord and prayed with such integrity and sincerity and God heard him. You know I once heard it said that God is not so much concerned with where we've been, He's more interested in where we are going. When we cry out to Him, He can come into an area of life that has been locked up, non-existent or distorted and release us. He can touch us in areas that no one else can.

Father God wants us to know Him as our Everything – our All. He wants us to know Him as Provider, Protector, Corrector, Encourager. He wants to train us up in His ways so that we will grow in His image.

For a very long time I didn't know God as my Father. I worked hard and even though I saw Him provide for others, I didn't really have an expectation that He would meet my needs or bless me. I knew what the Word said, but on the inside, I just didn't believe He would want to do anything for me. My life was filled with striving and pressure. So, I started to bring the matter before Him recognising that something in my life needed to change. I began to allow Him to show me how I had not received Him as Father.

Around about that time I was praying for the provision of a car. The vehicle I was driving was about eleven years old and it was wearing out. (In Australia we often drive vast distances to minister, so a reliable car is essential.) I can remember my mother had a dream one night. She said that I would be driving a new car of my choice and it would be debt free. About two weeks later someone phoned me (now remember this prayer request was not widely known). This person told me to go to a car yard, pick out a car and have the salesperson phone him. This phone call sent me into a complete panic. This was the answer to my prayer, but I was having difficulty receiving what the man had said.

In my heart, I kept thinking, 'What will this man want in return? People don't buy other people cars! Why would he do this?' I can remember being very spiritual about the matter and saying to friends, 'I will need to pray about this and see if it is the Lord's will.' One friend said, 'Well, if you don't want it, do you think he would let me have it?'

I realised that I had difficulty in receiving something that I hadn't worked for or earned. I felt unworthy. The Holy Spirit ministered to me in such a powerful way. He made me able to accept this gift from the Lord.

I went to the car yard and chose the very car I had desired for a long time. The man who purchased the car for me made sure I ordered the sports model. A few days later my new car arrived at my house. I was overwhelmed. This car represented so much more to me than a mode of transport. It was the provision of my heavenly Father. He gave me the very best. He gave me the desire of my heart. I did nothing to earn it.

My car has been such a blessing. It is a miracle, but it is also a testimony. The Father is wanting to lavish us with love (not just materially but in every way), and we need to be positioned to receive from Him. Where there has been the fruit of the curse of fatherlessness He wants to establish blessing.

Breaking the curse of fatherlessness

Deuteronomy 5:16 says,

> *'Honour thy father and thy mother, as the LORD thy God hath commanded thee; that thy days may be prolonged, and that it may go well with thee, in the land which the LORD thy God giveth thee.'* (KJV)

This is one of the Ten Commandments. When the Law was given to Moses, there was clear instruction to honour parents. Although this is 'Old Testament' the principle remains: life will go well for us in the areas in which we honour our parents. God blesses us when we honour our parents. That means there must be sense of honour in our hearts toward them.

Your father may have consciously or unconsciously caused you pain. The pain may be so deep that you don't even want to think about it. It may be difficult to honour him, but the truth is that this remains a principle of God. To really enter into relationship with Father God, we must walk in forgiveness and love toward our earthly father. (He may have passed away or moved away, but God requires us to come to the place of forgiveness and honour.)

Nothing is impossible with God. **He is able** to touch you and bring healing to your heart so that you **can** honour and **can** experience the joy He has for you. If you will but ask He will speak to you about this matter. He will minister to you. He will show you what He requires of you and give you the grace to follow through. He wants the curse of fatherlessness broken.

Psalm 68 verse 6 tells us that He sets the solitary (the orphan) in families. If you have never had a father, He is able to 'set you' into His family.

Each time I've ministered this message I have been led to have a man of God pray for those who have come forward to the altar. I have called upon someone with an anointing as a father in the natural and spiritual realm. As these ones have come and laid hands upon those who responded to the call, I have seen the Lord bring deliverance and healing. Blessing has begun to be established where curses had rested. The prayers have been simple yet effective. Many of those whom I've since seen have said that the Lord has led them into a place of forgiveness of their fathers, and even better relationships with those parents still alive. The blessing of a father brought the blessing of the Father. It broke curses. It restored and healed.

A few months ago a man shared a testimony with me regarding this message. He was present at the camp the first time I ministered this word. He responded to the call. Even though he is a highly successful businessman he knew he had to go to the altar. His father (who is no longer alive) loved him dearly but never gave him an encouraging word.

The man remembered that as a small boy he would strive to do well at soccer and all he wanted was to hear his father tell him how well he had done. Yet he never did. The night he heard the message he was prayed for and accepted the prayer in faith. Nothing dramatic seemed to happen to him. Yet, when I spoke with him more than six months later he said he had noticed blessings in areas that previously had not known blessing.

There was much more favour around his life and when he tracked back in his thinking he noted the blessings had begun after the camp. This is a powerful message. If you respond to it, then as with this man, it will change your life.

Simply by having a godly man – a father lay hands upon you and pronounce blessing, curses are broken or lifted and favour is established. The anointing breaks yokes and lifts burdens. You are released to succeed!

A prayer to break the curse of fatherlessness and establish God's blessing upon your life:

> 'Lord, I want to know You as **my** Father. I want to know You as Provider and Protector. Lord, I want to know Your correction and the safety of being in relationship with You. I ask You to break the curses that have come around my life as a result of fatherlessness. I ask You to heal me and to speak to me. I ask You to give me Your grace so that I can honour my earthly father. Lord, I want to know Your blessing upon my life, so in Jesus' Name, I ask You to do what is necessary to bring me to the place of walking with You as your child. Amen.'

Chapter 4

The Wells of Isaac

Hidden deep within the stories of the Old Testament lie principles by which the Kingdom of God operates. I call these principles **Kingdom ways**. If we choose to live by these laws then we prosper – we move forward, we advance and we experience great blessing.

Genesis 26 presents us with an account of Isaac and his journey toward destiny. This chapter shows us how a man of God dealt with all that stood between him and his call – how he handled the challenges that came before him. And, most importantly, how he chose God's way each time he was confronted with difficulty!

This story is a testimony for all believers. It holds a very important key for each one of us. You see, we face many of the same obstacles Isaac faced as he progressively entered into his call in God. Any man or woman who desires to fulfil his or her spiritual potential will face opposition. How we handle what comes against us will reveal our maturity. It will also **always** bring the opportunity to go to a new level in the Lord.

Let's look at the background of this story ... The Lord promised Isaac great blessing and inheritance because of His oath to Abraham, and Abraham's faithfulness to Him. Isaac was instructed to remain in Gerar. He tried to pass his wife off as his sister which caused him to be noticed by the King and subsequently brought Isaac under his protection. He planted crops. He cared for his animals. He put down roots in the land and God prospered him. In the midst of famine he reaped a harvest of that which he had sown – in the same year! **The blessing of Almighty God was upon this man.** Isaac became wealthy and powerful.

This caused the Philistines to envy him. They were jealous of his success. So, they filled up all of the wells of his father Abraham with dirt. They closed up what they understood to be the source of Isaac's provision.

In the Middle East wells are of extreme importance. They are given names and considered to be landmarks, because water is vital. It sustains life. (Even today it is common to see Bedouin moving around the desert from well to well.)

In a spiritual sense wells represent places where there is water to sustain us – to give us life. Wells can be actual places – churches or ministries from which we deeply drink; but mostly wells are the places which we dig within our own lives to hold and precipitate the flow of Living Water. John 7:38 says:

> *'He that believeth on me, as the scripture hath said, out of his belly shall flow rivers of living water.'* (KJV)

As believers, there are wells in our lives that must be dug to ensure the life-force of Jesus flows in us and through us – so that we are refreshed and sustained, but also so that we have the ability to refresh others.

Digging wells in the natural realm is hard work. It takes time and effort and there are no shortcuts. It is both repetitious and tedious. Digging wells in the spirit is just the same. Wells are dug when we do the same things over and over – time in the Word, prayer, obedience . . . over and over and over . . . day in and day out . . . with diligence and perseverance.

The Philistines hit Isaac where it hurt. They tried to stop up the flow of blessing by cutting off what they perceived to be the source of the blessing he walked in. They were unaware that the real source of Isaac's blessing was the God of Israel.

Isaac became so prosperous that the King requested him to leave town! You know, when you are obedient and God begins to bless you, there will be people who will become jealous. They'll speak against you and they'll reject you. Scripture says, *'And Isaac departed thence...'* (see Genesis 26:17 KJV). He didn't argue. He didn't defend himself or the blessing he lived in. He just moved on. In fact, he moved to the valley of Gerar. The King James Version says that in the Hebrew language the word 'valley' in this passage means dry valley. So, this was not a place where a man could easily flourish (in the natural). A valley is a place where there is limited vision. It's a place surrounded by barriers. Yet, this is the place God's man settled.

He set about reopening the wells of his father that the Philistines had closed up. His servants dug a well in the valley and *'... found there a well of **springing water**'* (Genesis 26:19 KJV). 'Springing water' quite literally means in Hebrew, 'living water'. So, in this place of limited vision, Isaac found living water!

Isaac didn't complain about the circumstances in which he found himself. What a lesson to us as we walk out our destinies. Even in the valleys we can find water that sustains.

The herdsman of Gerar claimed ownership of the well. So, Isaac named the well *'Esek'* which means 'contention and strife'. He dug another well. Again, there was a dispute over its ownership. Isaac called it *'Sitnah'* which means 'hatred and opposition'.

You know, the man of God didn't get involved in strife, he didn't retaliate, he simply moved on. He just kept going in his call. He didn't get side-tracked. He didn't fight in the flesh. He just kept obeying what he felt the Lord had said to him.

Isaac moved on and dug another well. He named this well, *'Rehoboth'* which means 'spacious'. He said,

> *'. . . For now the LORD hath made room for us, and we shall be fruitful in the land.'* (Genesis 26:22 KJV)

Isaac recognised there was something special about this particular well. There was a peace about this well that had not been present as he dug the other wells. He had broken through against his enemies. He was able to prophetically declare *'we will flourish in the land'* (NIV).

If Isaac had entered into a war of wills or a fleshly dispute at either Esek or Sitnah, he may never have reached his Rehoboth. He may have been side-tracked for years or he may have been taken off course completely.

Really the message here is **'Keep the strife out of your life'**. Isaac pursued peace even when it looked like it had cost him. I meet so many people all over the world who have such powerful calls, yet when opposition comes, they don't rise above the circumstances, they enter into strife. When you enter into strife you make a way for the enemy to operate through you and you open yourself up to demonic attack. **What came against Isaac was spiritual opposition and what will come against you as you walk in your call will be spiritual opposition**. Don't get into fighting people. Obey the Word – walk in love, pray for and bless those who give you a hard time. The enemy will find no opening in your life, you will be pleasing the Father and you will prosper!

If you learn how to hold your spirit well – how to stay in peace and victory in times of opposition and continue on in the vision, you will come to the place where the Lord has made room for you in the spiritual realm.

King David was one who knew great opposition throughout much of his life. In fact, there were times when his very life was under threat. He said of the Lord, *'... thou has enlarged me when I was in distress'* (see Psalm 4:1 KJV). David learned a valuable truth during the difficult times of his life. He learned that when he was in distress, when he couldn't control the circumstances, and when things happened to him that he didn't deserve, when he kept a right spirit his God would cause enlargement and increase to come around him and maturity to be worked within him.

David's testimony can be our testimony. You and I can say of the Lord, 'Thou has enlarged me when I was in distress. Through this circumstance You have brought growth to my life.'

King David was an extraordinary man. He held his spirit well by giving the highest place in his life to worship. He continually worshipped his God. David poured out his heart before the Lord daily. We would say, 'he was real with God'. Lastly, he chose to walk in forgiveness.

✣ ✣ ✣

Think back to Isaac the central character of this chapter ... the man of God who held his spirit well in the face of opposition. He was so centred on the covenant he had with God and so focused on his call, there was no place in his life for anger; there was no place for bitterness; and no place for revenge. **A revelation of covenant and an understanding of personal destiny made it impossible for him to hold offence in his heart**. He kept his eyes on God and kept walking forward in His purposes.

I'm sure that you have heard preachers say things like, 'circumstances can make you bitter or better'; or 'when life hands you lemons, make lemonade'. These sayings and others like them, sound a little silly, but actually present us with a great opportunity to live the way God would have us live. As we stride ahead into our destinies, there will come many occasions where we will have the choice to hold offence (to be angry with someone or even God) or to release and bless.

When we choose to hold offence ... the offence takes root in our lives. It becomes part of us and affects our attitudes. The offence is never far from our thinking. It is held close to our hearts and we become introspective and selfish. It brings limitations to relationship. (**No one wants to be around an offended person.**) Bitterness grows within us and everything we touch starts to be tainted with a spirit of offence where there was once a spirit of love. Our hearts harbour cynicism and criticism – and out of the mouth the heart speaks. Our spiritual life begins to be affected when we just can't get past what that person did to us.

Every undealt with offence is like a heavy stone we carry through life. The more offences we hold – the heavier our load becomes and the more energy we require simply to handle our load. We have little energy for the important things in life!

Some realities of the issue of offence

1. Most people who offend us aren't even aware of what they've said or done! (And when the offence is pointed out they are so sorry to think they have hurt us.) Others realise as soon as they've spoken or acted their behaviour has been offensive.
2. Scripture makes it very clear that we are to follow the path of love. We are to forgive, even as God has forgiven us. This is not an option. This is a directive from heaven. To choose not to release someone who has offended us (and the offence) is disobedience to the will of the Father.
3. All disobedience to the Word bears fruit. The fruit of holding offence is that we bind the person who has caused the offence to us with invisible cords of the spirit. So, wherever we go and whatever we do, we are taking the offence and the tie to that person with us. We are holding them in bondage!

4. Our prayer lives are affected (see Mark 11:25). The authority and power in our prayers diminishes.
5. We give the devil an opening to launch an attack.
6. The anointing we walk in is affected.
7. We find it difficult to hear clearly from the Lord.
8. We reap back offence (people begin to be offended with us).

There is only one way for the believer to live – and that is in love.

> *'...a prudent man overlooks an insult.'*
> (Proverbs 12:16 NIV)

If you take offence easily and are sensitive, then get over it! Change. Become a woman of the Word. Choose to forgive and you will find God's grace pours down around you and gives you the ability to walk out forgiveness. As with many of the things of the Lord, act in **faith first**, then **feelings will follow**.

> *'Let us therefore come boldly unto the throne of grace, that we may obtain mercy, and find grace to help in time of need.'* (Hebrews 4:16 KJV)

I can remember when I was first learning to ski. It seemed to be the hardest thing I had ever done. I flunked the beginner's class and almost hit a tree! Then I spent an afternoon trying to stay upright on my skis on the kiddie slope. (To make the situation worse, the friend who took me skiing had dressed me up in a pink parka and red balaclava.) She kept emphasising my need to keep warmly wrapped up. I really didn't care. I just knew I looked ridiculous and stood out in the crowd!

I was relieved when the slopes closed for the day. I was so pleased to carefully make my way up to the rest area. As I slumped onto a bench and endeavoured to get the contraptions connected to my boots off my feet, I felt like a failure. After all, I had seen three and four year olds flying down the slopes. Just when I was encouraging myself with thoughts like, 'hey Noela you can't be good at everything' a man approached me. He said something like, 'I saw you on the slopes today. You were sitting on the ground. In fact, every time I saw you, you were sitting on the ground.' Then he walked off laughing.

I was burning on the inside. I was so offended at what he had said. I kept thinking, 'didn't he ever have to learn.' You know that incident really affected me. I went back to my friend's home that night and couldn't sleep. I was so angry. Like most women I could remember what he said, how he was standing, even what he was wearing! The incident kept replaying over and over in my head. I couldn't seem to get the victory over this offence. I even thought, 'If he's there again tomorrow I'm going to give him a piece of my mind!

Well, the Holy Spirit spoke clearly to me that night and simply said, 'Noela, let it go.' As I came to the place of obedience, and forgave the man, I actually found the whole situation something to laugh at! When I asked the Lord why I had become so easily offended, He showed me the pride of my own heart. It had brought an opening for the offence to be lodged. I had become accomplished at everything I had ever set my mind to, and this had brought pride in my own abilities. I wasn't accustomed to failing. That day on the slopes I was faced with a sport that I obviously had no natural talent for.

Back to Isaac...

As blessed as he was in the 'spacious' place of Rehoboth God had more planned for His man. He wanted to take Isaac beyond any place of blessing he could imagine. So, from Rehoboth, Isaac *'went up'*. He travelled to Beersheba. He travelled to a new place and a new spiritual level and in that place God revealed Himself to Isaac in a new way. He declared who He was. He ministered to the fears in Isaac's life. He said He would never leave him. He promised Isaac blessing and destiny.

Often we think of the characters of the Bible as far more than human beings. Isaac was a flesh and blood man. He had walked through great opposition in life, found his Rehoboth and 'come up' to the place where God revealed Himself in a new way. God ministered to him personally in the area of fear. Do you think it was easy for Isaac to stand in the face of intimidation and jealousy? Do you think it was easy for him to hold his spirit well? He was just a person – like you or I. He chose God's way, and so God enabled him to gain victory over his fears.

Isaac built an altar to the Lord. He pitched a tent and his servants dug a well. Abimelech the King who had asked Isaac to move away visited him in Beersheba. He sought peace with Isaac because of the blessing of the Lord that was so evident upon his life. Isaac called the well at Beersheba *'Shiba'* meaning 'oath' or 'seven'. (Beersheba can mean 'well of the oath' or 'well of seven'.)

So, the Lord re-affirmed covenant with His man and he made his enemies to be at peace with him. He took Isaac way beyond what he could have anticipated ... all because he held his spirit well in times of great opposition.

Proverbs chapter 4 says:

> *'Above all else, guard your heart, for it is the wellspring of life.'* (Proverbs 4:23 NIV)

This is an instruction to protect the heart and its condition above all other things. This is not something we pray, it is something we do. The responsibility is upon us to keep our hearts with all diligence (see KJV). We do this by keeping watch over that which enters our hearts and by choosing to walk in love.

Isaac presents us with a picture of a man who overcame. His example stands as a challenge to every man and woman of God to choose to walk in the Spirit and not after the flesh. His testimony is of a God who promotes and blesses the one who pursues peace.

Each day you and I have the decision to choose life!

Scripture tells us how we are to handle offence:

> *'He who covers over an offence promotes love,*
> *but whoever repeats the matter separates close friends.'*
> (Proverbs 17:9 NIV)

> *'A man's wisdom gives him patience;*
> *it is to his glory to overlook an offence.'*
> (Proverbs 19:11 NIV)

See also the Lord's prayer in Matthew chapter 6. Verses 14 and 15 say:

> *'For if ye forgive men their trespasses, your heavenly Father will also forgive you: But if ye forgive not men their trespasses, neither will your Father forgive your trespasses.'*
> (KJV)

Chapter 5

Only One Thing Is Needful

'As Jesus and his disciples were on their way, he came to a village where a woman named Martha opened her home to him. She had a sister called Mary, who sat at the Lord's feet listening to what he said. But Martha was distracted by all the preparations that had to be made. She came to him and asked, "Lord, don't you care that my sister has left me to do the work by myself? Tell her to help me!"

"Martha, Martha," the Lord answered, "you are worried and upset about many things, but only one thing is needed. Mary has chosen what is better, and it will not be taken away from her."' (Luke 10:38–42 NIV)

Martha and Mary figured prominently in the life of Christ. They were friends of the Lord. He spent time in their home and loved them (as well as their brother Lazarus). In the Gospels we read of their relationship with Christ and one another. We see that although both of these women loved the Lord and desired to serve Him, they were actually quite dissimilar. Each expressed their devotion in different ways.

The first time we read of the sisters is in Luke chapter 10 (the passage listed above). Martha extended an invitation of hospitality to Jesus. Now, when we consider this passage of

Scripture there are two things to keep in mind. Firstly, Martha made the invitation. She was believed to have been the older sister (the woman with the authority in the household). Secondly, when she opened her home to Jesus, she was also inviting (by custom) all those that were with him. So, she was inviting the Lord, His disciples and anybody else who was travelling with Him at the time. I heard one preacher say that there could have been up to eighty people in Jesus' company that day! So Martha wasn't just asking Jesus home to dinner. She was inviting to her home a large group of people which would constitute catering something of the magnitude of a significant event.

Martha's heart had been to bless Jesus and minister to Him. She wanted everything to be just right, and, when the guests arrived, they quickly filled up her house. You know when you have a large number of guests in your home, they sometimes go into rooms you would prefer to keep private. They often touch precious things you don't want them to touch. Some don't respect what they ought to respect. Martha became 'stressed out'. She felt anxious and angry. She had expected her younger sister Mary to help with the preparations. She had expected her to help serve the guests, but her sister was sitting down listening to Jesus! No doubt Martha looked at Mary in exasperation thinking, 'Can't she see what needs to be done. Why is she leaving me to do all this work on my own!'

In frustration Martha approached the Lord and asked Him to tell Mary to help. Jesus looked straight at the one who loved Him so much and said, 'Martha, Martha, you are anxious and upset over the things that have to be done. You have been distracted even from My voice. You're angry with your sister because she has been sitting with Me listening to My word. Martha, only one thing is needed – only one thing is really important and that is hearing My voice. Mary has chosen that. It is the better part and will not be taken from her.'

Only one thing is needful and that is to hear the voice of the Lord. You and I could make a list of all the things we think we need, but really all we need is to sit and hear His word. We rush around going here and there; we do many things 'to minister to the Lord'; we are seen to be busy in service; yet, if we will but come before Him and listen to what He has to say, we will receive His strategy for every work; we will receive His plan for prayer; we will receive His direction; and something will be imparted into our spirits that could come no other way.

For many years I 'served' the Lord. I was really busy – often I was too busy to hear His voice. My prayer life was somewhat successful and I saw a measure of blessing on my ministry, yet I knew there was more. I began to seek the Lord in a new way. Rather than praying everything I knew to pray about an area of life or family that needed breakthrough, I began to wait upon Him. I would sit and listen for His direction as to how to pray. I found the more I did this, the more manifestation of answered prayer I received. I found that instead of praying through and pushing in the spirit, I was prophetically declaring what the Lord had told me was His will. I prophetically declared the Scriptures and words He gave me. A prophetic anointing was released upon my intercession. I knew I was praying what Scripture calls 'aright' so I knew the prayers would be effective. Boldness and faith entered my heart, because I knew the will of the Father.

You know, what you hear sitting at the feet of Jesus carries weight in the spiritual realm. One word from Him contains everything you need to walk out His will. His words are anointed words – they break yokes, they lift burdens and they release His miracle working power!

When I began to put aside some of the things that needed to be done – some of the things that made me anxious – just to sit at His feet, I began to operate more out of my spirit than out of my mind. My plans became streamlined in His presence. Answers to situations came when there was no earthly answer! New things were conceived in my heart by His Spirit. Through the listening I was changed – my desires and priorities changed.

Throughout my years of serving God I have read so many books on leadership and management. I've studied successful people and the habits they've observed to bring success (and these things can be good), yet really, success only comes one way – and that is being in the place before the Lord where you can hear His voice and obey His instructions.

John chapter 10 says that,

> *'...the sheep hear his voice; and he calleth his own sheep by name, and leadeth them out.'* (John 10:3 KJV)

The Lord speaks to us personally and individually because we are in relationship with Him. The more we listen for Him and to Him, the more we recognise His voice when He speaks. He has said,

> *'...his sheep follow him because they know his voice. But they will never follow a stranger; in fact, they will run away from him because they do not recognize a stranger's voice.'* (John 10:4, 5 NIV)

✣ ✣ ✣

The incident recorded in Luke 10:38–42 shows us the importance of hearing His word (above all else). His instruction or what He has to say is higher than any other thing! His word is His wisdom, and His wisdom will advance you in every situation. It will lead you to prosper in every area. Proverbs 8:10, 11 says,

> *'Choose my instruction instead of silver,*
> *knowledge rather than choice gold,*
> *for wisdom is more precious than rubies,*
> *and nothing you desire can compare with her.'* (NIV)

I've been seeking the wisdom of God for a long time. I don't just want to cry out to God in times of desperation, but I want to walk in His wisdom. If you seek wisdom when you need it, then the Father will provide it (James 1:5–7), but there is a higher way. You can have a piece of His wisdom to help you make a right decision in a time of pressure, or you can live in His wisdom daily. You can allow His wisdom to shape your life – to lead you forward along His paths. You can enjoy the fruits of peace and joy that only His wisdom bring. It is a choice.

Take a look at what the Word says about the wisdom of God.

> *'The Lord brought me forth as the first of his works,*
> *before his deeds of old;*
> *I was appointed from eternity,*
> *from the beginning, before the world began.*
> *When there were no oceans, I was given birth,*
> *when there were no springs abounding with water;*
> *before the mountains were settled in place,*
> *before the hills, I was given birth,*
> *before he made the earth or its fields*
> *or any of the dust of the world.*
> *I was there when he set the heavens in place,*
> *when he marked out the horizon on the face of the deep,*
> *when he established the clouds above*
> *and fixed securely the fountains of the deep,*
> *when he gave the sea its boundary*
> *so the waters would not overstep his command,*
> *and when he marked out the foundations of the earth.*
> ***Then I was the craftsman at his side.***
> *I was filled with delight day after day,*
> *rejoicing always in his presence,*
> *rejoicing in his whole world*
> *and delighting in mankind.'* (Proverbs 8:22–31 NIV)

Before God did anything, He brought forth wisdom! He placed that much importance on this aspect of His nature and ability to create what was formed in His heart. Wisdom stood with the Lord as He established the natural world. Wisdom became the craftsman at His side!

How much more should we see the need to have wisdom stand alongside us as we live out our Christian lives. How much more should we ask wisdom to watch over everything we do. How much more do we need wisdom – the Master Craftsman.

'Get wisdom, get understanding;
do not forget my words or swerve from them.
Do not forsake wisdom, and she will protect you;
love her, and she will watch over you.
Wisdom is supreme; therefore get wisdom.
Though it cost all you have, get understanding.
Esteem her, and she will exalt you;
embrace her, and she will honour you.
She will set a garland of grace on your head
and present you with a crown of splendour.'
(Proverbs 4:5–9 NIV)

The wisdom of God is not limited as men's understanding is. It is not hard to find! Begin to listen. Begin to ask the Father, 'What is wisdom in this situation? What would You have me do in this situation?' Wisdom will speak. It will call out to you with His instruction. Make this a part of your relationship with the Lord, and you'll begin to sense the Master Craftsman fashioning your life in a whole new way.

Wisdom says,

'I love those who love me,
and those who seek me find me.' (Proverbs 8:17 NIV)

The Book of Proverbs gives us so much understanding as to what the wisdom of God actually is and how we can receive it into our lives. There are 31 chapters in Proverbs.

Why not read one chapter every day – meditating upon the truths it holds and acting upon its instructions.

✣ ✣ ✣

Back to Martha and Mary . . .

By sitting at the feet of Jesus listening to His words, Mary chose the 'better part'. She exalted wisdom above works. If we read the records of interaction that took place between Martha, Mary, Lazarus and the Lord in John chapters 11 and 12 we will see why Mary chose the 'better part'.

John chapter 11 records the death and resurrection of Lazarus. Even though Bethany where Lazarus had died was only about 15 minutes walk from Jerusalem where Christ was, He waited some days before travelling to the grieving family. On His arrival Martha came out of the house to meet the Lord. She had a conversation with Him declaring her belief in who He was. Martha went back into the house and told Mary Jesus had come. Mary hurried out to the Lord. She fell at His feet. She was once again in that place of worship. Her Lord was deeply moved by her grief and He wept. He asked to be taken to the tomb where He requested that the stone be rolled away. Martha reminded Him that the body had been entombed for four days and would hold the stench of death. Jesus reminded her of His word that if she believed she would see God's glory. Then, He called the dead man to life.

Martha and Mary both loved the Lord. He loved both of them. Yet, Mary possessed an intimacy and depth of relationship that Martha didn't appear to walk in. This intimacy moved the heart of Christ to act on her behalf. It stirred Him to call a dead man back to life. Intimacy with Jesus causes Him to act on our behalf. It causes Him to intercede for us and act for us in a way that petition praying alone could not. Every heart cry from the one who walks in intimate relationship with the Lord is heard. Intimacy causes Him to release His miracle power and call to life that which has died.

John chapter 12 presents us with the last account we read of Jesus and His friendship with Martha, Mary and Lazarus. Shortly before He walked the Calvary Road, He went to be with this family where a dinner was held in His honour. Verse 2 tells us that '*...Martha served*'. We could say, 'Martha still served'. In spite of all that had taken place and all that she had seen, Martha still served. This seemed to be the only way she could express her devotion to the Lord, when He had called her to know Him and not just to serve Him.

While Lazarus reclined at the table with the guests, Mary took some costly perfume and poured it over the feet of Jesus. She wiped His feet with her hair and Scripture says that the whole house was filled with the fragrance. This young girl, believed to have been no more than eighteen years old, took the most precious thing she had and spilled it over her Lord's feet. Theologians believe that she probably used her wedding dowry to acquire the ointment (the cost of which in today's currency would be tens of thousands of dollars). Little did she know at the time, she was anointing the feet of Jesus to walk the road to the cross. She was led of God to perform a prophetic act the significance of which she would not know until she reached eternity.

From amongst all those who loved Christ, this young girl was chosen to anoint Him for His greatest act of obedience to the Father! She anointed Him for His high call. She ministered to Him in a way that no one else ever has.

The fragrance of the perfume lingered in the family's home. It permeated Mary's hair and hung heavy in the air around her. To her, the fragrance was the evidence of her love for her Lord. To others in the house, it was an offence. Judas spoke up and said that the money could have been used more wisely (even though inwardly he wanted the money for himself). To some her act of devotion would have appeared improper, with the implication that this young woman had a wrong relationship with Christ.

Mary walked in intimate relationship with the Lord and it cost her. This relationship cost her far more than the obvious financial outlay of the perfume. It cost her in the opinions of men and their judgements. That day as she poured the perfume over the feet of Jesus, she laid down her life for Him. It will be the same for us if we desire to walk in intimacy with Him. There will be a laying down of our lives, but there will also be a leading of His Spirit to minister prophetically – in ways which we will not fully understand. These acts of obedience and devotion will minister to Christ Himself.

Only one thing is needful . . .

We have been called to worship, not works. However, as we lavish love upon Him, He leads us to acts of service. These acts of service all bear fruit because they have been inspired of Him. They are all anointed and they all produce joy. We can work and ask Him to bless our work; or we can worship and go forth from that place in Him and serve in His grace.

- Martha invited Jesus to her home. Ministering to the physical needs of the Lord was her vision. She became angry when Mary didn't help – even speaking with Jesus about the matter. **Don't judge those around you when they are not doing what you think they ought to be doing to serve Jesus.**
- Martha judged Mary's relationship with the Lord. **Don't judge how others worship or serve the Lord.**
- Mary did not allow the pressures of men's opinions to move her. **She counted her relationship with the Lord as more important than misunderstanding and criticism.**

✣ ✣ ✣

We each determine the level of relationship we walk in with God. The level is not determined by our past. It is not determined by our circumstances. It is determined by us. We choose how deeply we want to know Him. He is no respecter of persons. He desires intimacy with each one of us.

Following is a prayer for those who know in their hearts they have been a **Martha**, but need to come to the place of being a **Mary**.

> 'Lord, I want to know You as Mary did. Forgive me for being a Martha – for being so caught up in all the things that need to be done. I love You Lord and I'm asking You to bring me into intimacy with You. Forgive me for judging the walks of others. Forgive me for comparing myself with others. Help me to sit at Your feet and hear Your instructions, so that I can go forth in effective service. Lord show me why I have a need to work to please You. Please deal with this area. Do whatever You need to do in me to bring me to the place where I know that I'm in You by grace alone. In Jesus' Name. Amen.'

Chapter 6

Associations That Bless

God has called us to relationship – firstly with Him and then with others. Most of us don't think all that much about the relationships we have with others. We don't think about the people that surround our lives and the impact they have upon us. Most of us don't think how we affect those we are in association with. The last chapter dealt with intimacy with the Lord. In this chapter I want to speak to you on the importance of right associations.

It's a simple thing to underestimate the value of being linked up or connected with the 'right people'. Oh, by the 'right people', I'm not speaking of wealthy and influential people. I'm speaking of people who do you good; people whom God brings into your life to challenge you, to minister to you and to bless you. These are ones who give you the opportunity to be a blessing to them. Every relationship in our life needs to be appointed by God – raised up of Him to be of benefit to both parties. Every association needs to be centred upon Him to bring Him glory.

There is a character from 2 Chronicles named Jehoshaphat who didn't understand the importance of right associations (this lack of understanding cost him dearly). 2 Chronicles chapters 17–21 tell us of Jehoshaphat's life. He was a king of Judah. The Lord established him in his kingship. He blessed him with wealth and greatness. Jehoshaphat had all that he needed in life. He was truly blessed and he honoured God.

Verse 1 of Chapter 18 says that Jehoshaphat had riches and honour in abundance (see KJV). There was nothing that this king lacked. He had everything anyone could ever desire. Yet, verse 1 continues, *'. . . and he allied himself with Ahab by marriage'* (NIV). Jehoshaphat went beyond what God had given him and entered into covenant relationship with Ahab the King of Israel. History records Ahab as having been an evil man who was insecure and easily threatened. (Self-preservation seemed to be the primary motive of his life.) His only interest was his kingship.

In the course of time Ahab approached Jeshoshaphat and asked for his support in going to war. Jehoshaphat, because of relationship, agreed. He was bound to Ahab through covenant, so there wasn't an option. However, the King of Judah urged the King of Israel to inquire of the Lord regarding the matter. Ahab didn't serve the Lord and he certainly wasn't interested in His will. However, for the sake of Jehoshaphat he gathered together four hundred prophets who all told him to go to battle for he would be victorious. Jehoshapat asked for another prophet. Ahab said there was one more prophet, but that he hated him (because he never said anything good). They called him. His name was Micaiah. He shared what the Lord had given him and was thrown into prison.

True prophetic anointing brings revelation. It brings God's counsel. It unfolds His purposes. If someone hates true prophetic anointing then this person has no desire to hear what God has to say.

In spite of Micaiah's prophetic insight, the kings went off to war. Ahab suggested that he enter the battle in disguise (so that he would not stand out in the crowd). He also suggested that Jehoshaphat wear his royal robes. Ahab was cowardly and he was a betrayer. He hoped that if anyone was to die in battle, it would be his friend the King of Judah.

If you read the account of this story in Scripture you will see that in the midst of battle Jehoshaphat was being pursued. His enemies thought he was the King of Israel. Jehoshaphat cried out to God and he was delivered. Ahab was wounded and died.

This unholy alliance ended in Ahab's death. He had manipulated Jehoshaphat. He had abused the covenant friendship. Only the grace of God saved Jehoshaphat.

The King of Judah returned to his palace. He was greeted by Jehu the prophet. He said,

> *'... Should you help the wicked and love those who hate the Lord? Because of this, the wrath of the Lord is upon you. There is, however, some good in you, for you have rid the land of the Asherah poles and have set your heart on seeking God.'* (2 Chronicles 19:2, 3 NIV)

Jehoshaphat was a good man. He desired to serve God, yet he had little discernment regarding the motives of those who approached him. He didn't understand the consequences of entering into wrong relationships.

I'll be honest with you, for a long time I didn't understand the importance of having right associations. Often I would befriend people from a heart of mercy. Sometimes I would befriend those who had no friends. It never occurred to me to ask the Father why they didn't have friends or if He wanted me to move on in there and walk with these ones. Many times I found this quite a costly exercise as I found myself to be set up, sold out or betrayed. There were times when these ones just weren't what they appeared to be. I suffered loss because of these associations. I was like Jehoshaphat. I loved the Lord, but I didn't really have a lot of discernment regarding the hearts of men.

I began to pray that God would raise the level of discernment in my life; that He would train me up to know the hearts of men; and that He would give me sensitivity to know His will for me in relationship.

Over the course of time I've found wisdom has grown and discernment has been developed in this area of my life, and, as part of this development, some interesting things have happened. Firstly, less unscrupulous people have approached me; and secondly, some really wonderful people have come around me.

Jehoshaphat didn't learn a lasting lesson from his association with Ahab. Later in life he made an alliance with Ahaziah King of Israel whom Scripture describes as having being *'guilty of wickedness'*. They entered into a business partnership to construct a fleet of trading ships. The Lord was so angry. He had one of his prophets declare to Jehoshaphat that as he had entered into this alliance, He would destroy what had been built. All of the ships were wrecked and never sailed.

When Jehoshaphat died, his firstborn son Jehoram succeeded him as King of Judah. When his kingdom was firmly established he had all of his brothers put to the sword, as well as some of the princes of Israel. Scripture says he walked in the ways of Ahab and he married one of the daughters of Ahab. Jehoram reigned in Jerusalem for only eight years. He died an early death being struck down by the Lord with a painful and lingering bowel disease. He died to no one's regret.

Jehoram became like Ahab and he ruled like Ahab. He became like that which his father had joined himself to. Friendship brings impartation. You influence your friends and they influence you. You become like them and they become like you. In this case, Jehoshaphat's son became like the one he was in covenant with. Ahab and Jehoram possessed many of the same traits. **The ones you surround yourself with can affect your children**.

The next king was Ahaziah who was Jehoram's youngest and only surviving son. It's interesting to note that Ahaziah also walked like Ahab. As well, he bore the same name as the King of Israel whom Jehoshaphat entered into a business agreement with. God brought about his downfall.

Associations and relationships carry spiritual significance and have consequences.

Relationship is an area that needs to be brought under the Lordship of Christ. It is an area that needs to be established in Him – not on emotional need or dysfunction. I want to ask you – What type of people do you attract? What type of people are drawn to you? Are they good, godly people of integrity? Or, are they people who will do you no good? 1 Corinthians 15:33 says:

> *'Do not be misled: "Bad company corrupts good character."'* (NIV)

Do you find that you are drawn into relationships with manipulating people? Do you feel abused by some of those around you?

The Word of God speaks many times in the Old Testament of fortified cities – cities strengthened by walls of protection. We hear a lot about taking down the walls of our lives so that we are open and vulnerable to others, but there is a need to ensure that positive walls of protection are maintained to ensure defence against the works of the enemy. It is no different in relationship. The walls are the boundaries that define the various relationships we enter into. They also protect us from abuse.

People who have suffered abuse and have not yet been healed have had the walls of their lives broken down. They have often been violated over and over. Some have even said to me, 'I feel like I'm wearing a sign. I just seem to attract abuse!'

There are many forms of abusive control – emotional, physical, verbal, spiritual, and financial. Each one of these forms of abuse is designed to take away the power of the abused by control and manipulation. Thus, the walls of the one who is violated are broken down. Sometimes they don't say no when they should say no. Sometimes they shouldn't come under what they come under. Brick by brick the walls of their lives are dismantled – until they have no sense of personal boundaries and feel weak and defenceless.

Boundaries are important to God. We read in Joshua that He told the children of Israel the boundaries of the land that He had given them to possess. We read of Saul being removed as king because he over-stepped his authority and walked in the boundaries of another's call. We read in the New Testament of boundaries for marriage, family and employment ... So, it is clear, that it is the will of the Father for us to have proper boundaries in place around our lives.

If you have been abused, ask the Father to give you a Nehemiah anointing to re-build that which has been broken down in your life. Ask the Holy Spirit to inspect the walls and give you His strategy to rebuild that which is broken down, to remove the rubble that has accumulated and to re-inforce that which is built but weak. Ask Him to show you how to build towers in your walls from which you can stand and see impending attack. Ask Him for the strength to stand against intimidation while you build. Ask Him for the grace to forgive those who have mistreated you. He is the Teacher and He will instruct you how to fortify your life in a godly way.

If you've been controlled and not been healed, then you will become a controller. If you have not forgiven and have judged your abuser, then you will reap back control. The Holy Spirit will teach you how to break patterns of control. He will even show you when to confront control and when to simply walk away. He is even able to break the fear of being controlled! He can set you free completely, so that you will have no expectation of being abused. Whom the Son sets free is free indeed!

More than this, He can teach you how to recognise control and side-step it. You can outwit every plan of the enemy without causing hurt. Remember, many controllers really believe they have your best interests at heart, so don't even know they are controlling!

When you build your walls under a Nehemiah anointing, the Lord will ensure that there are gates to receive those He sends into your life. You are the gatekeeper. It's up to you to ask the Lord, 'Father did you send this one to me?'

When you allow Him to set clear boundaries around your life, you actually become a 'safe' person for others. They feel secure around you and know that you won't manipulate them to do your bidding and that you won't impose your will upon them. Because you have been released, it becomes easy to release others to be themselves. Healthy relationships begin to be built and great fruitfulness comes forth.

Partnership in the Gospel

It is so important to be linked in with the ministries God has called you to share in. Partnership in the Gospel is a spiritual and practical relationship of love and support. It is ordained of the Lord as a means of fulfilling the Great Commission. Every ministry has those whom God has called to link up with, support, and pray for the ministry, so that there is an enabling to fulfil the specific tasks God has assigned.

The Apostle Paul understood this valuable spiritual relationship. The Philippians were his partners in the Gospel. In fact, the Book of Philippians is a partner letter – from Paul's heart to those who stood with him.

I remember as a little girl spending a great deal of time with a particular aunt. I would visit her house often. She was a believer and was a partner to many of the most effective ministers of that time. These men were winning thousands of souls to the Lord in each crusade. She honoured these men. She prayed for them. Every room in her house seemed to be littered with evidence of her partnership. There were magazines, reports and calendars from those ministries all over the house! She sent them offerings to help in the work and she really felt a part of what they were doing.

I was not yet a believer, but I knew certain things about my aunt. There always seemed to be such a spirit of victory about her. She was involved with miracle ministries – and often miracles happened for her! She gave liberally, but was always abundantly provided for. She walked in the favour of God! So, when I was born again at nineteen, it seemed the easiest thing in the world for me to enter into partnership with the men and women of God whom I was directed to. I may never meet some of them, but I'm linked in. I'm in relationship with them. I'm a part of their ministries and I'm sharing in the fruit.

Partnership is relationship. It is a commitment of heart to uphold a ministry, and is based on the spiritual principle of agreement (see Matthew 18:19), and so produces spiritual strength. It means that you are believing two things:

1. That you will share in the fruitfulness of that ministry both here and in eternity. You have a share in the ministry of every soul saved and every person ministered to. Paul said to the Philippians,

   'Not because I desire a gift: but I desire fruit that may abound to your account.' (Philippans 4:17 KJV)

2. That the anointings upon the minister/ministry will begin to be established in your life.

Over the years I have received so much impartation of anointing from the ones I'm joined with in partnership. There has come increase and adding of anointing to areas of ministry. At times I hear people complaining that partnership is just a way for ministries to meet their budgets. This may be true for some ministries, but not all. Ministers who have a revelation of the relationship of partnership are not just looking to get blessed, they are looking to bless. They are opening up their ministries so that we can be an important part of their commission. I challenge you that every time you receive a partnership form, pray over it, and ask the Father if He has ordained you to link up with this one in the spirit realm.

Chapter 7

An Assigned Task

'No one knows about that day or hour, not even the angels in heaven, nor the Son, but only the Father. Be on guard! Be alert! You do not know when that time will come. It's like a man going away: He leaves his house and puts his servants in charge, each with his assigned task, and tells the one at the door to keep watch. Therefore keep watch because you do not know when the owner of the house will come back – whether in the evening, or at midnight, or when the rooster crows, or at dawn. If he comes suddenly, do not let him find you sleeping. What I say to you, I say to everyone: "Watch!"' (Mark 13:32–37 NIV)

We all have an 'assigned task' – a specific call from the Lord to fulfil whilst on earth. This call can only be fulfilled within the framework of a broader call to steward or manage the life the Father has granted us. In this chapter I want to share with you the importance of managing well that which He has entrusted into our care. We will speak about time and money, and I want to leave you with the challenge of stewardship with excellence – being the best you can be and doing the best you can do!

Understanding time

The concept of time and its process was created by God. He is the Author of time. Time exists for a reason. It has a purpose. It is a measurement for our lives and that which takes place around us.

Just as God has placed time frames within the natural world, He has set times in the spiritual realm. Whilst He lives in eternity (and has set eternity in our hearts) He chooses to work His purposes out on the earth through a system of time. In the natural world, time operates from moment to moment, and stretches out to become minutes, hours, days, months and years.

Time reminds me so much of money. It can be wasted or spent wisely – even bringing a return if it is invested well! Each one of us has been given 24 hours a day to manage, that is, 24 hours each day in which to glorify God. If we give our time to Him and incorporate the principles of the Word regarding time into our lives, then we will see time expand. The Holy Spirit will breathe upon our time. He will begin to order our time according to His priorities – cutting away the unnecessary and the unfruitful. He will begin to deal with procrastination, so that we'll become diligent. He will convict us of the areas in which we waste time. He will give us His creativity and ability to expedite all that needs to be done. **He will stretch time for us** so that we are able to accomplish far more than we ever dreamed! (Read the story in Joshua chapter 10. It tells us that the sun stopped in the middle of the sky for about a full day, so the Israelites could win victory over the Amorites.)

Often we don't do what we know we should do, because we 'just can't see how' performing a little task will really make all that much difference. I can remember as a child learning music. For about the first year I practised on the keyboard every afternoon after school for 30 minutes simply because I was made to! I couldn't see how the scales and chords I was learning would ever sound like music. It seemed all so disjointed and it wasn't all that much fun. I had lost sight of my dream to play well. I had lost sight of why I was doing what I was doing. I had lost my sense of purpose.

Purpose produces power! It produces the motivation to do whatever it takes to see a goal accomplished. It produces the dedication and diligence required to achieve. It brings the knowledge that moment by moment you are advancing toward the fulfilment of your vision. Purpose pushes you beyond procrastination to action; it brings the mental and emotional ability to keep going during tough times and the diligence to persevere.

Time is not wasted when we have purpose – and we should have purpose in every area of our lives. We should all have goals. Goals help us stay on track as we press forward to our destination. They are steps along the way and as we reach them we are spurred on further. Goals are established out of vision – what we see ourselves doing and being. We need big goals and little goals, long-term goals and short-term goals.

I want you to take some time to think about purpose. What is the vision you have for your family? What is the vision you have in God? What is the vision you have for your career?

When you have a vision, begin to think about what it will take for you to walk in that vision. What will you need to sow or give into that vision? Will you need to learn some new skills? Will you need to change? Ask the Lord to show you what it will take.

Sometimes women tell me they feel a little heavy and have decided to lose weight. You know most times when I see them again they look the same. Nothing has changed. Yet, there are others who say, 'I'm going to lose weight and this is how I'm going to do it.' When I see these women again, most have been transformed.

- **They have vision.**
- **They have set goals.**

- **They have purpose and the purpose has produced passion.**

If you keep your life in line with His purposes, you will have the time you need to do all that is required – in fact you will achieve more. If you submit – body, soul and spirit – to His Word then you will not waste time or run out of time. You will manage your time well.

Cut away the unnecessary. Unless it is an emergency, you do not need to spend an hour on the phone each day to a friend! It does not profit anything to sit and watch hours of TV. In the light of eternity it is not important to go out each morning to have coffee with friends.

Start to streamline your life and bring every area into Divine order. If you over-eat, then stop and take care of your body by planning a balanced diet. If you're untidy, then start to clean up. God does not bless a mess. If you are a hoarder, then go through your house right now, room by room, and take every item that is no longer of use (e.g. broken or unsafe) straight to the dump. Straighten up your linen cupboards, kitchen cupboards and clothes cupboards. Get a bag and fill it up with things that you haven't worn for years. Take them immediately to a charity shop. If you have a problem with your conversation, clean it up. Bring your words into line with the Word.

Start to think out some type of routine that will work for you (not so tight that you think you're living in a concentration camp). Think about the responsibilities in family and career that you have that are set and can't be moved, and then think about the times of day when you are most alert. Think about creative ways to streamline your time – things like doubling up some recipes so that you have extra meals to freeze, writing a grocery list before shopping, do all your errands in one trip. Let the Holy Spirit help you create time for the really important things in your life.

I've talked earlier about the importance of time with the Lord. It is imperative that we give time to Him. It should be a practice for every believer to spend some time praying in tongues – building ourselves up in our most holy faith. Praying in the Spirit lifts us above the natural and it places a clarity and strength within us that nothing else can.

You also need time for yourself. I can hear some of you saying, 'what's that?' We all need recreation time. This is time when we are re-created. It's time when we are refreshed and are able to relax without the pressures of being someone's daughter, wife, mother or grandmother. This time is different for every person. For me . . . it's things like going for a walk in the bush, or going to the ballet – something that ministers to the depths of my being.

Divine interruptions

God is a God of order, yet there are times when He interrupts the order of our lives with the unexpected. He leads us into an unplanned place of ministry or blessing. He gives us Divine appointments. He sets the scene and then brings us on the scene, so that we are at the right place at the right time to meet the right person!

Divine appointments are set in heaven. They sometimes come at inconvenient times. They are always meetings that leave lifelong impact.

I can remember once boarding a flight in Auckland, New Zealand. It was a Friday morning and I was flying home to Brisbane. I was really tired. I had arrived in Auckland on the previous Monday and spoken at a prophetic conference on the Tuesday, Wednesday and Thursday. As I sat down in the passenger seat, I remember thinking, 'Oh Lord, it would be so good if the seat next to me remained empty.' Then there was an announcement over the loudspeaker. We were waiting for one more passenger who was in transit from another flight. Not long after the announcement, a girl came bounding down the aisle. She was a backpacker and had a huge bag on her shoulders. She collapsed into the chair next to me. The girl was a university student who had deferred her studies to travel. She was so excited about going home that she began talking immediately!

I asked her where she had been. Her reply to my question was something like, 'I've been searching for God . . . ' Only a few minutes later I led her to the Lord. I quietly asked if she would like me to pray with her. The girl boldly answered 'yes' and offered me her hand. In that three-hour trip the young girl not only gave her heart to Christ, she received a foundational class on Christianity, and we prayed for her family! This was an appointment set up by the Father. He heard her cry and met her need.

I have experienced many Divine appointments in various parts of the world. Sometimes they have been set up to magnificently meet a need in my life. Jesus had many Divinely appointed encounters. When He met the Samaritan woman at the well, she had a Divine appointment with the Lord. Jesus laid aside His usual travel route to pass through Samaria and meet with this woman.

God has Divine appointments for you! He has men and women whom He has ordained to be a blessing to you and be blessed by you. Be willing to lay aside your plans to walk in His plans!

> *'See then that ye walk circumspectly, not as fools, but as wise, Redeeming the time, because the days are evil.'*
> (Ephesians 5:15, 16 KJV)

To 'redeem the time' means to 'buy it back' or 'set it free'. There is only one way to redeem time – to maximise the time God had given us stewardship over – and that is to place it under His Lordship and loose His anointing into the measurement of time!

Money, money, money

> *'The law of the LORD is perfect, converting the soul: the testimony of the LORD is sure, making wise the simple. The*

> *statutes of the* Lord *are right, rejoicing the heart: the commandment of the* Lord *is pure, enlightening the eyes. The fear of the* Lord *is clean, enduring forever: the judgments of the* Lord *are true and righteous altogether. More to be desired are they than gold, yea, than much fine gold: sweeter also than honey and the honeycomb. Moreover by them is thy servant warned: and in keeping of them there is great reward.'* (Psalm 19:7–11 KJV)

After time, the most obvious part of life which we have been given stewardship over is our material world. This includes property and goods, as well as money. For the purposes of this chapter I want to focus on financial stewardship. Money means different things to different people. For some, money is security, for others it is power, and others still, it is food on the table. But, as with time, money can only be managed well under the Lordship of Christ.

The Word of God has much to say about money and its use. It presents us with spiritual laws that govern Biblical economics. As we study the Word we begin to see God's purpose for money and our minds become renewed by His statutes. Poverty thinking is challenged and dealt with as we begin to see Him as our Source. We begin to be moved to align our financial lives with His Divine order.

Anointed financial stewardship begins with recognising God as Source. We may have an income from a job, a pension, or investment returns, but we are not limited to what that means of provision brings us. When we have the revelation in our hearts that God is our Source of provision, we are lifted beyond the natural to a place of supernatural provision. As covenant men and women we see that God brings us opportunities for financial advancement that the world does not present.

> *'But thou shalt remember the* Lord *thy God: for it is he that giveth thee power to get wealth, that he may establish*

his covenant which he sware unto thy fathers, as it is this day.' (Deuteronomy 8:18 KJV)

He gives us the power to get wealth. He gives us the creativity and wisdom for financial increase.

We are promised the blessings of the Abrahamic covenant through Christ Jesus. Just as these blessings overtook the father of our faith, so they will overtake us if we accept that they are ours and believe for them to be manifest in our lives! Take a look at what Deuteronomy 28 says about these blessings. All these blessings are ours! The Lord takes pleasure in the prosperity of His servant (see Psalm 35:27).

As you manage the finances God has placed in your hands remember that **God is source** and **you are not limited to earthly means**. If you obey the biblical principles of money management, you will prosper. These principles will undergird all that you do financially, and 'set you up' for advancement. These principles will bring you out of the slavery of debt into financial prosperity.

The foundation for our stewardship is tithing. Tithing is giving a portion (one tenth) of the increase God gives us back to Him. It is taken off the top and is given to Jesus to set before the Father in worship and thanks for His provision and blessing. Many people say that tithing was required under the Law and that we are under grace – therefore we are not required to tithe. However, tithing was instituted before the Law which makes this argument invalid.

Our tithes are given to God as a step of obedience to the Word; thanks that He has provided; and faith that He will endow us with the tither's blessing (see Malachi 3:10–12). A lot of people tithe faithfully every week, but there has to be an element of faith as we give our tithe to Him. There has to be an expectation that we will walk under an open heaven.

The Word instructs us to bring our tithes into the 'storehouse'. For most people the storehouse is the church that they attend. However, the storehouse can be actual ministries, e.g. for the believer in prison, the storehouse may be a

TV ministry; for the shut-in, it may be a teacher of the Word they continually hear on cassette tape. A storehouse is a place of supply. It is a place that stores provision. So, the place where you tithe should be the place where you receive provision. This will be the place where you receive the bulk of your spiritual guidance, counsel and teaching.

The Hebrews in the Old Testament always made a declaration as they gave their tithes. Don't just drop your tithe in the offering bucket as it goes by, worship the Lord with your tithe. Pray over that cheque or cash amount before you give it. Open up the Word and declare the promises of Malachi 3 over it. Expect your tithe to make a way for you.

There are specific aspects of giving spoken of in Scripture as being the will of God for our lives. We are clearly told that when we give to the poor we are lending to the Lord. We should all pray and ask the Father what He would have us do for the poor. We should all be investing in the Great Commission – giving to the Gospel so that others can hear the message of the cross. We should all be giving what the Old Testament calls 'praise offerings' to the Lord. These are offerings which we are not compelled to give, but rather, offerings we choose to give from a heart of love for Him.

I want to speak with you for a moment about investments. An investment is something that you set aside today for the sake of tomorrow. A seed that is sown is an investment. It is buried in the ground and looks forever lost. Yet, in good time, it germinates, grows and produces a plant (see John 12:24).

An investment is something that brings a return. In financial management you have both earthly investments and spiritual investments. An earthly investment may be something like an investment property, shares or a superannuation fund. A spiritual investment may be financial offerings or seeds sown for which you are believing for a return (see Mark 4), or perhaps regularly helping someone pay off a debt, believing that you will be enabled to supernaturally pay off your debts. The Kingdom of God is based upon seed time and harvest – the principle of investment.

It is not wrong to expect something back! John 3:16 shows us that God gave His son. He invested the life of His son in expectation of receiving many sons. Let God pull your finances under His wisdom. Watch as He releases His power into impossible situations. Watch as He prospers you.

Chapter 8

Jehovah Jireh

At the beginning of this year I received a revelation of Jehovah Jireh that has transformed my life...

For many years I had waited upon the Lord for His timing to attend a particular minister's conference. Each year when I received the conference brochure in the mail, I would sense the Spirit say, 'not yet'. Then last year when the details of the conference were posted to me, I knew 'it was time'. It was one of those 'you know that you know that you know' experiences a believer sometimes has.

I completed the registration form and sent it back and began to announce to people that I would be attending the conference. I was stunned to receive a letter back from the ministry involved telling me there were no more spaces – that Australia was only allotted so many seats and they had already been filled. It went on to say that even if someone cancelled out, there would be no way I could go. I went back to the Lord a little confused as I had really believed I was meant to attend. I went to my friends and said, 'I must have really missed it this time'. I was certain the Lord had called me to go.

I was still wondering what had happened, when weeks later 'out of the blue' my office received a phone call from the ministry that was hosting the conference asking if I still wanted to go. I had to get back to them within a day if I wanted a conference seat! There were only a couple of weeks remaining before the event which was being held on another continent! And, I had re-scheduled my diary for that time. This whole thing had become a step of faith and obedience to what I had sensed God earlier say.

The conference was to be held in Fort Worth, Texas. When we called the ministry, we found that the venue was way out of town. I couldn't catch a taxi, bus or train to the sessions. They told me the only way to go was to hire a car. I made every endeavour to find a lift, but, because the event was now so close, no one had room for me. I really didn't want to drive in the United States, as they drive on the opposite side of the road to us. The steering wheel is on the left. The driving conditions are very different from what I am accustomed to.

I exhausted every avenue to try and find a lift to that conference. In the end I just went back to God and left the matter with Him (planning to be on that plane in a matter of days)! When it seemed like there was no way for me to attend, I received an email from a friend in Hong Kong. She had heard from another friend that I was planning to go to Texas (you know how Christian circles are). Anyway, she said she had a friend in Fort Worth whom she had been in contact with. She had gone ahead and organised accommodation for me. All I needed to do was to telephone the woman and tell her my flight details, so she could pick me up at the airport.

Toward the end of the email (it seemed almost as an afterthought), my friend wrote something like, 'By the way, my friend in Texas has a limousine service and she is off work for those three days. She will make sure you get to the conference.' I was overwhelmed. I had never experienced the provision of God in such a way. I had asked Him for a ride and He had provided much more!

I got to ride around in a very large black limousine. This blessing represented a valuable lesson that the Spirit was wanting to teach me. I had asked for a ride and He gave me the very best that the earth could offer. As I sat alone in the back of that vehicle I was prompted to get down on my face before the Lord. So, I lay flat out on the floor of the limousine and just worshipped Him. I asked Him to forgive me for the times I had limited Him and 'pulled Him down' to what I could see as possible.

The people I stayed with in Fort Worth were a Divine appointment. Both they and I knew that God had brought us together. I also got to minister during those few days in Texas (an unexpected treat). As well as all that, I sat under anointed preaching and teaching! God had done exceedingly abundantly above all I could have asked or thought. I came home changed and challenged by His awesome ability to provide.

The Lord will provide

Abraham is called the father of faith. He had so much faith in the ability of his God to provide that which He promised, he was lifted above a natural walk. When God made a covenant with Abraham (see Genesis 15) He told him to 'look up'. Abraham looked up at the heavens and saw the stars, and he believed Jehovah. He was enabled to receive every promise of the Father.

Two more times Scripture records Abraham looking up. Both of these times are in Genesis 22 – the chapter that reveals Jehovah Jireh – the God who Provides. Abraham was tested. God didn't test him to torment him. He tested Abraham, because He wanted to bring His man to another level of faith. He gave him an opportunity to obey His instructions. Abraham had a choice. He didn't have to obey. He chose to obey and that act brought him to a greater revelation of his God and a greater level of faith.

Every time the Lord gives you a promise or an instruction He requires a response. If you receive what He says, then He will provide all that you need to take you to a new level in Him. Every test is an opportunity!

Abraham took his son – his only son Isaac and set out to sacrifice him in obedience to God. On the third day which the New Testament shows as resurrection day Abraham 'looked up'. On the first two days of the journey Abraham 'had died'. He had laid down his son. He had experienced a death experience to his flesh. On the third day, he 'looked up'. He looked up to heaven, he looked up to the promises of God, he looked up to the faithfulness of God. In the 'looking up' Abraham received all of the grace and strength needed to obey the Lord. Scripture says that Abraham *'looked up and saw the place in the distance'* (Genesis 22:4 NIV). He was not looking at a physical place. He was looking at a place in the spirit – a place of victory, a place of promise. He had come through confusion, fear and the grief of laying down his son. Now, all he saw was the faithfulness of God.

He instructed his servants to wait while he and the boy went to worship. He said that because his obedience was his worship. He told the servants that both he and boy would return. This was a statement of faith. When the boy asked where the sacrificial animal was, Abraham simply replied, 'God will provide'. Abraham laid his son upon the altar he built and placed the firewood on him. He lifted the knife and was about to sacrifice Isaac when God called to him. At that moment Abraham came through to a new level of relationship with his God. The Lord stopped him from plunging the knife into his son's body. Just then Abraham 'looked up' and saw the provision of God. It was a ram in a thicket which he took and sacrificed to the Lord.

> *'So Abraham called that place The LORD Will Provide. And to this day it is said, "On the mountain of the LORD it will be provided.'* (Genesis 22:14 NIV)

Abraham needed to be in the place of God's appointing before he was able to receive God's provision. It is the same for us. For Abraham 'the place' involved a physical place as well as a spiritual place. Abraham received an instruction from the Lord. He didn't question the will of God. He simply obeyed and as he obeyed he was changed, he was prepared to receive the provision of God.

When God gives you a promise or instruction, He waits for a response. If you say yes to His word, then as you start out in obedience, He will take you on a journey to the place of receiving His enabling to possess His best. Along the way, you will be required to lay down your life – to deal with fleshly emotions so that you can rise up in the spirit and receive provision from His Spirit. When you have reached the place (His appointed place of provision), you will look up and begin to worship, then you will see His magnificence in bringing that which you need.

Believing and delcaring

Abraham gives us two keys to seeing the provision of God in our lives. He started out in faith in response to the word of God. He just started walking. The Book of Hebrews says that Abraham reasoned that God was able to give him back his son. In his mind he knew that God could raise Isaac up again. But, really, Abraham just started walking.

When the Lord gives you a promise, just start walking. Expect God to give you the details along the way. Don't try and work out how He could bring what He has promised to pass, just obey.

When questioned by Isaac as to where the sacrificial animal was, Abraham declared, *'God himself will provide the lamb for the burnt offering'*. He was declaring, 'God is going to do something totally supernatural here. Watch and see. He is going to provide according to His ability'. We, too, must maintain a declaration of faith when the ones around us question where our provision is, before it is made manifest.

The Lord has provided a ministry

My life is full of testimonies of the Lord's provision. I have seen Him provide over and over. I have seen Him bring to pass my dreams and His promises. I can remember when He first spoke to me about my call to England. I didn't know anyone in that land, yet I understood that if I accepted the call, He would somehow make a way. I would often take a map of England and place it on the floor. I would stand on it and declare in faith that in the timing of the Lord I would preach the Word in that land. He prepared me for that aspect of my ministry and at the right time He opened His doors.

There is always a waiting time in God. It is a time when striving and human effort are put to rest. It is a time when we prove His promises. It is a time when we learn to stand in faith in spite of a lack of change in the natural realm. Abraham knew about waiting. He waited for the manifestation of his promised son for a very long time. Romans 4:20–21 says,

> *'He staggered not at the promise of God through unbelief; but was strong in faith, giving glory to God; And being fully persuaded that, what he had promised, he was able also to perform.'* (KJV)

His faith stand gave glory to God. It blessed the Father that Abraham believed Him. When we wait patiently in faith it blesses the Lord. It brings glory to Him, because we are a testimony of trust in His integrity.

Patience is a fruit of the spirit. It is developed by choosing to set our hearts upon Him. Galatians says that Christ came into the world *'in the fullness of time'*. He came at just the right time. God will bring to pass that which He has promised us at just the right time – when conditions are perfect and when we are prepared to receive what He has for us. Patience begins with a decision – 'I will hold my spirit in peace and I will trust the Lord.' Patience is one of the outward signs of maturity.

> *'Cast not away therefore your confidence, which hath great recompense of reward. For ye have need of patience, that, after ye have done the will of God, ye might receive the promise.'* (Hebrews 10:35, 36 KJV)

This verse indicates that you are not going to receive the promise without patience! It is an important part of the process of faith and when you have allowed its work in your life, you will receive.

Chapter 9

Building an Ark

Matthew 24 speaks of the end times. In this chapter Jesus instructs His disciples about the various things that shall occur in the earth before the Second Coming. At one point Jesus likens the last days (the days in which we live) to the days of Noah.

> *'As it was in the days of Noah, so it will be at the coming of the Son of Man. For in the days before the flood, people were eating and drinking, marrying and giving in marriage, up to the day Noah entered the ark; and they knew nothing about what would happen until the flood came and took them all away. That is how it will be at the coming of the Son of Man.'* (Matthew 24:37–39 NIV)

According to the Word, the earth in Noah's time was corrupt in God's sight and full of violence. Scripture says that the people had corrupted their ways. Lawlessness and rebellion prevailed. However, Noah remained righteous and blameless before the Lord. Despite the wickedness that surrounded him, **he walked with God**, and because he walked with the Lord, he heard His voice. Through all the noise and all the unrest that surrounded him, **he heard the Lord.**

Noah was instructed to build himself an ark, that is, to make a dwelling place for his family that would provide **protection and provision** in the day of Divine judgement. The Lord gave Noah specific instructions as to the dimensions of this ark, the building materials he was to use, and exactly what he was to bring inside the ark.

So, Noah built an ark.

'Noah did everything just as God commanded him.'
(Genesis 6:22 NIV)

He laboured for many months by faith. He didn't really understand why he was doing what he was doing. He just knew he was being led of God. His friends and neighbours thought he had completely lost the plot. Everyone who passed by saw him working on the ship in his backyard.

When the ark was completed according to its heavenly blueprint, Noah brought his loved ones and the animals God had specified into the ark. The rains came down and flooded the earth in judgement. Noah and his family remained safe, whilst the remainder of mankind perished.

The earth was filled with wickedness in Noah's time. Scripture tells us that the thoughts of men's hearts were evil all the time. It was as if man was bent toward evil and took pleasure in depravity. (That sounds pretty much like the time we live in.) Yet, Noah remained righteous before the Lord. He remained blameless in his generation. And, he was granted a place of protection before the Lord.

In spite of the darkness of his day, Noah **walked with God and heard His voice**. In this day, we need to be **walking with God and hearing His voice**. We need to be leaning close, so that we can hear His instructions as to how to build for ourselves and our families an ark of protection.

Noah's ark was an actual physical vessel that he constructed from earthly materials. It was built to meet the specific dimensions the Father had given and was made according to His instructions. The ark was huge. Its dimensions were great, so it took many months to build.

The ark that each of us is called to build is a spiritual place. It is a place that will keep us safe at all times. It will carry us through times of God's judgement upon the earth. It will ensure that we are kept safe in the perfect will of God who orders our days and that we are in the Lord's care through every attack of the enemy.

Before you even contemplate building an ark there are certain things that you will need to know:

- The Lord Himself will give you His blueprint to enable you to build an ark of protection that will keep you and your families safe. The specifications He gives you will be unique. He alone knows what you will face in the days ahead. He alone knows the dimensions of relationship in Him that will keep you in victory. Don't look at how others 'build' in the Spirit. Ask Him to give you the plans He would have you work from.
- Building is hard work. It is labour. To build a place in the Spirit that will bring protection is going to take time and effort. You build by faith, and that means you can't always measure your progress by what you see! You build by obedience, and that means following the directions of the Lord without question. When we talk about an 'ark' (a place of safety in relationship with the Father), I often think that some people just want to build a life raft – something that is barely adequate, but stable enough to save them in a time of emergency. Others want to build a luxury cruiser – something that looks so good to others, but can't stand up to the storms.

How we build an ark

We build an ark in the spirit by taking the materials God has given us: **prayer, the Word, the name and the blood** – to build a relationship with Him that will keep us safe.

Prayer is a vital part of any believer's relationship with the Lord. It is imperative that we pray. When we pray we are pouring out our hearts before Him; we are bringing our petitions to Him; and we are declaring our trust in His great power. However, there is a way to pray that builds in the Spirit. I'm not speaking of praying in tongues that according to Scripture builds us up in our most holy faith. I'm speaking of taking Scripture and praying it out – praying it over our lives to build the truth of that Scripture into our lives and around our lives. The Word is anointed. It is a living force and as we declare it in prayer, we are praying out the will of God – His highest and His best for us. He will lead you to the scriptures He would have you pray out over your own life and that of your family. He will give them to you. They will be a part of His heavenly blueprint and these scriptures will mean so much to you, especially when you have your own testimony of preservation in a dangerous situation.

I can remember years ago hearing the testimony of a very well known minister. Troops from his nation were sent to a war torn area of the world in an attempt to bring peace. The soldiers were sent to a dangerous place in a dangerous time. This particular minister felt that the Lord had given him the instruction to 'build an ark' for these men and women and believe for their safety. Every morning he prayed out Psalm 91. He believed in his heart that the truth of the words he was praying would cover each soldier and that God would honour His word. When the troops arrived home, a great to do was made of the fact that from the thousands of soldiers sent to this area, there were no casualties. A coincidence? I think not. God's word does not return to Him void!

God responds to faith. He responds to our trust in His ability. We really do receive what we believe for. Take the scriptures He gives you – ones like Psalm 23 and Psalm 91 and begin to pray them out aloud over your household! You will come to the place where you know them so well that you don't have to read them. You can just declare them and live in the security of His Word!

The Word

When I gave my heart to the Lord, I can remember just being delighted in the Word. I just loved the Word. One night as I was reading a particular verse, it seemed like the words of that scripture just jumped off the page at me. It was as if they were highlighted above all else on the page! I didn't have the natural understanding to know this was a *rhema,* but I knew that God was giving me this verse. It was His word to me.

A *rhema* is a particular verse or scripture that the Spirit of God has highlighted to you at a particular time as opposed to *logos* which is the general word of God.

The scripture He gave me was Isaiah 26:3:

> *'Thou wilt keep him in perfect peace, whose mind is stayed on thee: because he trusteth in thee.'* (KJV)

That night that verse became a very part of me. I knew that if I kept my mind on Him, then He would keep me in peace. That verse has kept me in the peace of God for over twenty years now. When something comes to try and pull me out of the Lord's peace, I just need to declare that verse in faith and get my mind back on Him.

God will give you scriptures to build with. He will give you parts of His Word that will live within you and become personal truth to you. Use these scriptures to construct a strong relationship with Him.

Become a hearer and doer of the Word. Make a decision that whatever you see in the Word, you will by His grace obey. Even if you don't understand it, and even if you don't like it, begin to build truth into your life.

The name

> *'Therefore God exalted him to the highest place and gave him the name that is above every name, that at the name of*

> *Jesus every knee should bow, in heaven and on earth and under the earth, and every tongue confess that Jesus Christ is Lord, to the glory of God the Father.'*
>
> (Philippians 2:9–11 NIV)

We need to understand something of the authority that is released at the name of Jesus (and we need to use that authority). When we use His name, we are not declaring by our own human name, we are declaring by the Highest Name! Even the very act of declaring in the midst of adverse circumstances that **Jesus is Lord** brings change in the spirit realm. It begins to pull circumstances under His Lordship. His name brings His authority.

The moment you begin seriously to build an ark in the Spirit, you will encounter opposition in the spirit. Like Noah, you may experience ridicule by those around you. People may say that you've gone right off the track. Like Noah, you may need to learn to just keep building. The authority of the name gives you the strength to stand during every challenge, and to keep building in obedience to the Father.

When the enemy comes to you as an accuser and speaks of your shortcomings and weaknesses, remind him you are a Christ-ian – you are in Christ. Begin to preach to him about the name. He will just want to run away and you will literally feel the authority of the Name rise within you.

The blood

There is nothing more powerful than the blood of the Lamb. It is the precious covenant blood that binds us to God. Every ancient civilisation operated by covenant – by binding agreement. In the western world, we don't understand what covenant really is. Contracts are often breached, broken and annulled. Men break their word, break their promises and look out for number one (which is totally contrary to covenant relationship).

In ancient civilisations men would enter into covenant with someone who had a strength or asset which they didn't possess. A covenant is a binding agreement for both parties, usually sealed in a ceremony, for example the covenant of marriage. It's more than an agreement, it's like a binding oath, which should not be broken. Through the agreement they would receive that strength, but also bring some predetermined asset to the covenant. In the covenant ceremony, the blessings for keeping covenant were listed and the curses for breaking covenant were listed. The agreement was sealed in blood.

The concept of covenant began in the heart of God. He is a covenant keeping God. Scripture says that He does not lie or change his mind (Numbers 23:19). He has cut a covenant with us through the blood of Christ (Hebrews 10:16–23).

Understanding covenant and the power of the blood of Christ is the only way to successfully build a relationship with the Father that becomes an ark. The blood of Christ makes you a victor. Even if you have always felt like a victim, revelation of the blood of the Lamb and what it has purchased for you, will cause you to live as a victor – one who has entered into the victory of Christ through the covenant. You won't do anything from a victim mentality. You'll do everything from a victory mentality. When the devil comes to tell you that you'll never build an ark, you'll be able to stand in victory and say, 'I can do all things through Christ who strengthens me'. When he comes to say that you are all alone and that no one understands, you'll be able to stand in victory and say, 'My God will never leave me or forsake me'. Victory (and all of the covenant blessings of God) will be sown in your spirit.

Begin to declare the power of the blood. Declare a blood covering over your family and everything you possess. State the covenant blessings of preservation and protection. Take communion often – remind yourself and the devil that you are a covenant woman and whatever you need you will receive from the Father. As you partake of the emblems in thanksgiving and worship receive His strength to build an ark that will bring glory to God!

Chapter 10

May It Be To Me As You Have Said

In an earlier chapter I spoke of an 'assigned task' – the fact that God has called each of us to some individual purpose, and through this purpose to bring Him glory. As we walk out our lives this purpose is held in our hearts through vision. Vision sustains us and keeps us moving in His paths.

Vision is conceived in our hearts by the Holy Spirit. It is sown deep inside us as a seed of potential and fruitfulness. It germinates by faith – as we receive the vision God has for us and surrender to His purposes. It grows to maturity by obedience – consistently saying yes to His will.

A seed of vision carries the anointing. It holds power to sprout forth and mature, because it is a seed of God. And, as such it carries His creativity and His ability. The seed of vision sown by the Spirit **cannot** germinate by the flesh. It **cannot** develop and reach maturity by the flesh. It is a supernatural seed! It cannot be seen by men. The seed of vision that God sows develops according to His timetable and is marked with Divine favour, right timing and miracles.

God has a seed of vision for each one of us! He has a seed which He desires to sow down deep inside us – a picture of what we can be in Him and what we can do for Him – a seed of fruitfulness. A vision of life empowered by His Spirit, lived in faith, glorifying His name. A life filled with unspeakable joy. So, how do we receive the vision God has for us? The answer is in the Word of God.

Luke Chapter One tells us of a godly young woman named Mary. She was engaged to Joseph. One night an angel appeared to the young woman and told her she was highly favoured of the Lord. She felt fearful and confused at the sight of the heavenly messenger and the words which he brought. He told her not to fear, for she was called to bear a son of great destiny. She immediately asked how this could come to pass as she was unmarried. The angel told her the child would be conceived of the Spirit of God and He would be the Son of God. He told her that even her barren relative Elizabeth would bear a child. The angel declared that nothing was impossible with God.

When God comes to sow a seed of vision in our heart, it will be an 'impossible' seed. It will sound impossible. It will be physically impossible. There will be no way His vision can come forth through human means.

Mary gives us keys as to how to position ourselves to receive vision from God, and how to respond to His word. She answered the angel sent from God with two simple sentences. She said,

> *'I am the Lord's servant ... May it be to me as you have said.'* (Luke 1:38 NIV)

We know that she was highly favoured of the Lord. She blessed the Lord with her life. When we bless Him with the way we live, then we too are highly favoured of Him. We become trustworthy servants.

We become just the type of person God is able to entrust with His will – ready to receive vision from heaven. Mary responded to the vision God had for her with great humility. She declared that she was His servant. To do His bidding was her greatest desire. Then, she made a statement of faith. In spite of the 'impossibilities' of the angel's word, she said, *'may it be to me as you have said'*. The seed of vision was sown in her heart. The Christ-child was conceived in her womb. Conception took place the moment Mary received the vision God had for her. She held the vision safe in her heart and nine months later she held in her arms the promised child.

When God sows a seed of vision it must be protected. It must be watched over and kept safe. Sometimes this will mean holding the seed in your heart for some time before telling others.

In the 1980s I was working in a church as a pastor. I can remember one morning going to minister the Word at a meeting in another district. During the altar call at that meeting, one of the ministers present came to tell me that he had a word from the Lord for me. I can remember being a little agitated as my focus was upon praying for those who had come forward to the Lord. I asked him to write down the word and slip it into the pocket of my jacket as I kept moving along the prayer line.

After the meeting I travelled back to church and was sitting in my office. A friend called to ask how the meeting had been. He had been praying for me that morning and a scripture kept coming to his mind. He told me the scripture and I wrote it down. When we had finished our conversation I immediately looked up the text. Then, I suddenly remembered the piece of paper the pastor had placed in my pocket at the meeting. I took it out, and was amazed to see it was the same Scripture passage as my friend had just given to me.

I opened my Bible to the passage and began to read. It was Jeremiah chapter 1 – the calling of Jeremiah as a prophet to the nations. I read verses 1–10, all the while thinking, 'this is for me?' After reading, I looked up to heaven and said something like, 'Lord, you have got to be joking. There must be some mistake. I could never be a prophet to the nations'. The words were barely out of my mouth and I turned my gaze back down to my Bible. My eyes fell upon verse 12. It was the word of the Living God. He was speaking to me. He said,

> *'You have seen correctly, for I am watching to see that my word is fulfilled.'*

There was such a presence of God in the room. It was still and quiet. He had presented me with a high call and I knew at that moment He required a response. I didn't see how this could be. I was a fairly quiet person and didn't think I had much of great value to say. I thought of prophets as being very bold and fearless people and I was bound by fear and intimidation. Yet, I knew He had spoken, and that day I said, **'Yes'** to the prophet's call.

I held that vision in my heart and watched in faith as it germinated within me. I sensed changes taking place around and within as I moved forward to become the woman who could walk in the vision. I allowed Him to place His desires within me for the nations. It was as if I was expanding to accommodate what was growing on the inside. Insight and discernment grew upon my life. The prophetic word rose on the inside of me. I even began to dream in the night seasons.

On the outside, it seemed nothing much had changed. No one suddenly came up and said, 'this woman is called to be a prophet'. The seed within me was hidden from men until the right time. Then when 'the fullness of time' came, my call came forth. I knew there had been a commissioning in the spirit. It seemed like all of a sudden those around me said, 'We really believe you have a prophet's call'. Then people began to refer to me as prophetic. Then there were some Divine appointments to bring the word of the Lord to prominent people. The Lord had conceived a supernatural call by supernatural means. He had brought the call forth in His way and His time.

God has a vision for you! He has a plan so powerful for you to fulfil. It will bring you such joy. To do His bidding will become your passion. Position yourself before Him and ask Him to conceive within you His purpose and then when it is made clear, say '**Yes!**'. Don't be concerned with the how or when His vision will be birthed. Respond in faith. He will do all that is needed to make you the woman that can stand in the vision. He will open doors that no man can close. He will make a way where there is no way.

He just wants availability. He desires ones who will walk in His purposes in faithfulness – ones whom He can entrust – willing vessels. So many times we concentrate on what we can't do and what we don't have, instead of looking to Him who is able to do all things and give all things! In coming into my call, I had to learn to place every human thought down before His Throne. When I considered my weaknesses, I had to look to His strength. When I heard what others said about me, I had to choose to listen to what He had said about me.

God will choose whom He will choose! Men look on the outward, but God looks at the heart. There may be many others 'qualified' in human terms to do a great job in your assigned task. Yet, if they are not called, they will achieve little for eternity. There will be no grace and no anointing. I had to learn a long time ago to get my eyes off people and onto God! Be willing and obedient and He will bring you into your call.

Not ability, but availability

In 1990 I went to minister in the Solomon Islands east of Papua New Guinea. This trip impacted my life deeply. I will never forget one incident which God used to forever change my heart.

One night after a meeting I was returning by canoe to the island on which I was staying. It had been a wonderful evening. Many lives had been touched by the Lord. I sat in the canoe (which was really just a tree that had been hollowed out) and stared up at the stars. The night sky looked so beautiful. There were no lights as there would be in my nation, so the heavens were dark and clear. I could just make out the island we were travelling to. It lay ahead across the water, and I could see the outline of the palm trees along the shore gently moving in the breeze.

It was a still night. It was very quiet. All I could hear was the sound of the young boy sitting behind me rowing as the oars sliced through the water. Another boy stood at the front of the canoe. He was holding a small lantern out over the water. It was low tide and he was guiding us through the coral reefs.

I was overwhelmed at the presence of God. It was as if He had enveloped me in the vastness of His being. I thanked Him for the privilege of ministering the Word that night. I felt so delighted to be in His will. I started to speak to Him from my heart. I wanted to know why He had called me to the Solomons. I seemed to face so many difficulties. Culturally it was unacceptable for a woman (particularly a single woman) to minister the way I had. The heat was at times quite unbearable. It made me feel so weak. There were places that I couldn't travel to simply because I was a woman. Yet, He had chosen me. I couldn't help but ask Him why He didn't choose some of the young men I knew. Surely they were physically stronger and surely it would have been more culturally acceptable for them to preach in the land ... As I sat in the canoe, His answer came clearly into my spirit. He simply said, 'I sent you here because you were available'. The words penetrated deep into my heart. They brought a priceless revelation to me that He will always use what is made available. That is His way. That is how He works. He delights in choosing the foolish things to shame the wise and the weak things to shame the strong.

The constant cry of the Father is, 'Whom shall I send? And who will go for us?' The greatest thing we can say to the Lord is, 'Here I am. Send me! I surrender to Your purposes, and whether You choose to send me across the street or across the world, I say "**Yes**"'.

When I accepted Christ as a teenager I never dreamt He would take me around the world. Over the years He has written His vision upon my heart. He didn't give it to me all at once. He gives it as I'm able to receive it and walk in it. He gives it to me as I'm able to rejoice in it.

Let Him unfold His purposes for your life. Be faithful to fulfil what He lays before you and He'll increase your authority and responsibility. He has chosen you. He has called you. He has anointed you. John 15:16–17 says:

> *'You did not choose me, but I chose you and appointed you to go and bear fruit – fruit that will last. Then the Father will give you whatever you ask in my name. This is my command: Love each other.'* (NIV)

When you're walking in your call, you will bear fruit! There is no doubt. You will be 'abiding' or linked into Him and so you'll have tremendous power in prayer. You'll be praying His will from a right heart. You will be motivated by His love for a dying world, and passion will fill your life.

An army of women

Right now across the earth God is raising up an army of women who shine. These are ordinary women who serve an extraordinary God. These are women of the Word who know their God. They are like the 'men of Issachar' whom Scripture describes as being ones who understood the times and knew what had to be done. They walk in prophetic insight and discernment. They maintain a 'gratitude attitude' toward their Heavenly Father. They know how to pray. **They are women who shine**.